Sound and Meaning

The Roman Jakobson Series in Linguistics and Poetics

C. H. van Schooneveld, Series Editor

≋ What Makes Sound Patterns Expressive?

The Poetic Mode of Speech Perception

Reuven Tsur

Duke University Press   Durham and London 1992

© 1992 Duke University Press

All rights reserved

Printed in the United States of America

on acid-free paper ∞

Library of Congress Cataloging-in-Publication

Data appear on the last printed page of this book.

Contents

Preface

This is a study in Cognitive Poetics. It takes its departure from the "mysterious" intuitions laymen, poets, and academic investigators have about the perceptual qualities and emotional symbolism of speech sounds. It attempts to answer questions that have been of great concern for literary theorists and critics as well as for linguists and psychologists. Its interest focuses on issues that have traditionally puzzled critics, who frequently offered ad-hoc explanations that would hardly hold water in a test of consistency. The answers here are drawn from linguistic and psychological research and have certain claims to consistency. In this sense, the present work may be called interdisciplinary.

People have "mysterious" intuitions such as the notion that front vowels like /i/ and /e/ are somehow higher than the corresponding back vowels /u/ and /o/, even when pronounced on the same fundamental frequency; that front vowels are somehow brighter than back vowels; that consonants like /p/ and /t/ are harder than /m/ and /l/; that languages like French, in which such sounds as *-on -eur* abound, are somehow more "beautiful," more musical than those languages in which such sounds as *pf* and *ts* abound; and so forth. Jakobson and Waugh discuss such intuitions under the heading "The Spell of the Speech Sounds." This book investigates their nature and source.

Having said this, I should explain that I come from the discipline of literary theory and have recourse to the tools and findings of other disciplines in attempting to answer questions in literary theory in which I have been entangled for many years. During the past few decades an enormous breakthrough in speech research has occurred, and much knowledge relevant to the above issues has accumulated. Only a very little of it, however, has reached the community of literary critics and theorists. This naturally raises the question, what kind of readers did I have in mind when writing this book. On the one hand, I certainly include speech researchers on whose work I have liberally drawn. On the other, I intend this work for literary theoreticians and critics, with whom I share so many of the problems to be solved.

Chapter 1, "How Do Sound Patterns Know They Are Expressive? The Poetic Mode of Speech Perception," accounts for the perceived affects of speech sounds by relying on the findings of the Haskins Laboratories' researchers concerning the "Speech Mode" and the "Nonspeech Mode" in aural perception. In the latter, the perceived natural noises or musical tones are very similar to the acoustic signal that conveys them. In the former, the perceived phonetic category is restructured, or "recoded," into abstract phonetic categories and does not reach awareness. The plosives /b/ and /g/, for example, are more thoroughly recoded than the sibilants /s/ and /š/. That is why we can tell from mere introspection that the acoustic signal that cues /s/ has a higher frequency than /š/; but we cannot tell that the only difference between /ba/ and /ga/ is that the frequency of a small section is higher in the acoustic signal of /ga/ than in that of /ba/. This work assumes there is a third, "Poetic Mode" of speech perception in which some rich precategorical sensory information is subliminally perceived, which is the source of the "mysterious" intuitions concerning speech sounds. It explains, for instance, the double—hushing as well as harsh—quality of the sibilants, the relative height and brightness of front vowels as compared to back vowels, the relative hardness of voiceless consonants, and much more.

Chapter 2, "On Musicality in Verse and Phonological Universals," uses Jakobson's model of children's acquisition of the phonological system of their mother tongue to explain the source of musicality and aesthetic quality of certain speech sounds and sound patterns. It offers a model to explain the differences between aesthetic and nonaesthetic instances of phonological regression. The referential use of speech sounds is typically nonemotional; the nonreferential use of sounds is, typically, emotionally loaded and used by children as sound gestures. In poetic language we have, typically, sound patterns in which both kinds of uses converge. Speech sounds later acquired for use in the child's arbitrary referential sign system serve longer in nonreferential babbling; these are the more emotionally and aesthetically loaded sounds, whether "beautiful" or "ugly." When acoustically continuous and periodic, as French *-on* and *-eur,* they are frequently perceived as beautiful; when abrupt and aperiodic, as German *pf* and *ts,* they are frequently perceived as ugly; as sound gestures, they are used to express unpleasant emotions, as in *pfuj.* This chapter explores the special uses of "beautiful" sounds in French Symbolist poetry; it also attempts to account for the "musical" equivalents sought out by Hebrew and Hungarian translators of Verlaine's "Chanson d'Automne."

Chapter 3, "Some Spatial and Tactile Metaphors for Sounds," explores certain basic intuitions concerning sounds in the nonspeech mode. Why do we perceive faster vibrations as thinner and higher than slower vibrations? It cannot be a reflex conditioned by familiar musical instruments: on the piano, the faster sound vibrations ought to be perceived as "right-wing," the slower ones as "left-wing," whereas on the cello, the faster ones ought to be perceived as "lower" than the slower ones. To make sensory sound-information reliable to the cognitive system, we recode it either into a spatial matrix (in the nonspeech mode), or into abstract phonetic categories (in the speech mode). The present chapter attempts to formulate the "rules" according to which nonspeech sounds are recoded into a spatial matrix.

Chapter 4, "Rimbaud's 'Voyelles,'" discusses this sonnet that became notorious for arousing in many readers a feeling of some mystic insight by associating each vowel with a color. Most studies tried to explain (away) this sonnet by discovering some hidden key, ranging from Rimbaud's colored spelling book, through the symbols of Alchemy and the Cabala, to the blazon of the female body. Even the structuralist conception of global homologies between sensory modes—largely embraced throughout this work—cannot do justice to the poem's uniqueness. This chapter uses the perceptual qualities of speech sounds, or of articulatory gestures, to account for the feeling of mystic insight by following the affects of the metaphoric attributions.

Chapter 5, "Psychoanalytic or Cognitive Explanation?," mainly considers methodological problems. It compares the relative merits of a cognitive and a psychoanalytic approach to issues related to the emotional symbolism of speech sounds. On the one hand, I shall defend the application of psychological theory to literature against Wellek and Warren's statement: "The psychology of the reader, however interesting in itself and useful for pedagogical purposes, will always remain outside the object of literary study." On the other hand, I should not take for granted that psychoanalytic theory in general, and inferences from psychopathology in particular, generally illuminate literary response and the emotional symbolism of speech sounds. In this respect, the discussion may have implications far beyond the scope of the present inquiry. In literary criticism, in particular, we find this problem to be rather acute. Some critics uncritically dismiss psychoanalytic theory as completely irrelevant to the business of criticism, and some critics adopt it—no less uncritically.

Perhaps the most important attempt to offer a psychoanalytic account of the issues discussed here is Iván Fónagy's work during the past few decades. Therefore, I am using his work as a paradigmatic example of the approach under examination. This chapter maps out the possible relationships between the aesthetic, the cognitive, and the psychopathological processes. I suggest that both the poetic and the psychopathological processes interfere with the smooth working of the same cognitive processes, the former for aesthetic purposes, the latter for psychopathological. However, arguing for aesthetic affects by relying on psychopathological disturbances is illegitimate: it turns a partial identity into a complete identification. Some of the mechanisms underlying Freud's *Psychopathology of Everyday Life* are considered from this perspective. Finally, the relative merits of the two approaches are considered with respect to a stanza by the great Hungarian poet, Attila József, discussed by Fónagy.

The title piece, chapter 1, originated in a happy coincidence. When I was first exposed to the Haskins theory of speech perception, I suddenly realized that the process of recoding the acoustic stream of information into a phonetic stream may serve as a hypothesis that can account for quite a few phenomena of sound expressiveness which have puzzled many literary theorists and critics. I had a similar insight concerning the relevance of Jakobson's model of children acquiring the phonological system of their mother tongue. This insight serves as the basis for chapter 2. I have not attempted to cover all the issues relevant to either the expressiveness of speech sounds and musicality in verse or to speech perception and the acquiring of the phonological system by infants. Hence, a certain disproportion in favor of these models may be observed. For the present edition I have updated certain issues in light of recent experimental work.

Finally, I wish to express my gratitude to Professor Alvin M. Liberman, who made it possible for me to spend eight months at the Haskins Laboratories, New Haven, for an instrumental investigation of my theory of the rhythmical performance of poetry. I wish to thank Professors Bruno H. Repp and Robert G. Crowder who read parts of my work, and Professor Iván Fónagy who reviewed the manuscript over several years and made insightful comments. I do not wish to imply that they approve of any part of my work, only that they helped me very much. I am also indebted to the members of the Cognitive Poetics Workshop at the Katz Research Institute for Hebrew Literature, who discussed with me in detail substantial parts of the present work.

What Makes Sound Patterns Expressive?

They Are Expressive? The Poetic Mode

of Speech Perception

Expressive Sound Patterns

Children often ask: "How does the dog know that barking dogs don't bite"? Similarly, it seems worth asking: May we attribute to dogs and sounds just any property we like, or is there something in the *nature* of dogs and sounds that warrants the attribution of these properties and renders their behavior consistent? Literary critics and ordinary readers usually have strong intuitions about the expressiveness of sound patterns in poetry. A vast literature exists on the subject; however, much of it is ad hoc, arbitrary, or skeptical. "It is precisely critics interested in the meaning and idea-content of poetry," says Hrushovski (1968: 410), "that feel some kind of embarrassment toward the existence of sound organization, and attempt to enlist it in the service of the total interpretation. As against this approach there are critics and theoreticians who deny all in all the very existence of specific meanings attributable to specific sounds."

In what follows I shall adopt Hrushovski's approach, according to which the various language sounds have certain general potentialities of meaningful impression (412) and can be combined with other elements so that they impress the reader as if they expressed some specific meaning (411). My claim is that these general potentialities—which I shall refer to as combinational potential—have firm, intersubjective foundations on the acoustic, phonetic, or phonological levels of the sound structure of language. More specifically, I shall rely on a simplified version of the mechanism as put forward by Liberman and his colleagues at the Haskins Laboratories, by which listeners decode the sounds and recover the phonemes.

Hrushovski claims that much of the dispute over whether sound can or cannot be expressive comes to a dead end because the issue is treated as if it were one phenomenon. "As a matter of fact, there are several kinds of relations between sound and meaning, and in each kind the problem is revealed in different forms" (412). He discusses four kinds of such relations: (a) Onomatopoeia; (b) Expressive Sounds; (c) Focusing Sound Patterns; (d) Neutral Sound Patterns. The main business of this book concerns the second of these relations, but my discussions will have some implications for the first. Hrushovski describes expressive sound pattern as follows: "A sound combination is grasped as expressive of the tone, mood or some general quality of meaning. Here, an abstraction from the sound pattern (i.e. some kind of tone or 'quality' of the sounds is parallel to an abstraction from the meaning of the words (tone, mood etc.)" (444).

Traditional poetics has important things to say about how "tone, mood etc." are abstracted from the *meaning* of the words. But how are they abstracted from the speech sounds? In this chapter I shall look into some possible sources of the "tone" or "quality" of the sounds and the way that tone or quality is grasped in relation to an abstraction from the meaning of the words (tone, mood, emotion, etc.). One important aspect of the issue is that sounds are what I call "double-edged"; that is, they may be expressive of vastly different, or even opposing, qualities. Thus, the sibilants /s/ and /š/ may have a *hushing* quality in one context and a *harsh* quality to varying degrees in some others. Hrushovski quotes Poe's line

> And the silken, sad, uncertain rustling of each purple curtain

where the sibilants may be onomatopoetic, imitating the noises; or they may reinforce—or be expressive of—a quiet mood in Shakespeare's sonnet:

> When to the sessions of sweet, silent thought
> I summon up remembrance of things past,
> I sigh the lack of many a thing I sought,
> And with old woes new wail my dear time's waste.

My argument relies on the assumption that sounds are bundles of features on the acoustic, phonetic, and phonological levels. The various features may have different expressive potentialities. The claim I shall elaborate is that in different contexts, different potentialities of the various features of the same sounds may be realized. Thus, the sibilants /s/ and /š/ at *some* level of description may have features with noisy potential and others with hushing potential. In Poe's line the former is realized by the contents, in Shakespeare's quatrain the latter.

At the beginning of Fónagy's article on communication in poetry (1961), statistical methods are applied to the expressive correspondence between mood and sound quality in poetry. This work is of particular interest for at least two reasons. First, it does not investigate the relations of sounds with specific themes, but with highly generic moods: tender and aggressive. Second, it does not consider these moods in isolation, but as a pair of opposites whose mutual relations may be treated in terms of more/less rather than in absolute terms. The data Fónagy presents are illuminating and highly suggestive. In six especially tender and six especially aggressive poems by the Hungarian poet Sándor Petőfi,

> the majority of sounds occur with the same relative frequency in both groups. All the more striking is the fact that the frequency of certain sounds shows a significant difference in both groups. The phonemes /l/, /m/, and /n/ are definitely more frequent in tender-toned poems, whereas /k/, /t/, and /r/ predominate in those with aggressive tone. For some reason, precisely these sounds seem to be the most significantly correlated with aggression, either positively, or negatively. (195)

The phonemes /m/ and /n/ have a similar negative correlation with aggression in poems by Hugo and Verlaine; /l/ is overwhelmingly tender for Verlaine, but not for Hugo. The voiceless stops /k/ and /t/ are significantly less frequent in tender poems by Petőfi, Verlaine and Hugo, and Rückert (Hungarian, French, and German poets). So, this distribution is surely not language-dependent. It would be interesting to know, to what extent if at all, "double-edgedness" is responsible for the equal distribution of other sounds in both groups of poems, owing to conflicting features' canceling out each others' influence (I shall try to answer this question later on). As for vowels, Fónagy mentions Macdermott who, through a statistical analysis of English poems, found that dark vowels are more frequent in lines referring to dark colors, mystic obscurity, or slow and heavy movement, or depicting hatred and struggle (Fónagy, 1961: 194). From this summary, one might expect to find a greater frequency of dark vowels in aggressive poems than in tender ones. Fónagy's investigation of Petőfi's poetry reveals that this is indeed the case (for the other poets, he gives only the consonant distribution). Whereas dark vowels occurred in Standard Hungarian 38.88 percent of the time, in Petőfi's aggressive poems it was 44.38 percent, and in his tender poems 36.73 percent. We receive a reverse picture from the distribution of light vowels. In Standard Hungarian they occur 60.92 percent of the time, whereas in the tender poems it was 63.27 percent, and 55.62 percent in the aggressive poems. While these deviations from Standard Hungarian seem to be convincing enough, one might reasonably conjecture that the correlation between aggressive mood and dark vowels may be even more compelling. The point is that the results may have been "contaminated." A poem may have an especially tender mood and still refer to dark colors (which, in turn, would have induced the poet to use words with dark vowels). The list of tender poems examined by Fónagy suggests that this may be the case in his corpus. Two of the tender poems seem to have dark atmospheres (or themes, at least): "Borús, ködös őszi idő" ("Dark and Foggy Autumn Weather"), and "Alkony" ("Dusk"). Statistical methods in poetics do not seem to be very successful in handling such multidimensional contrasts and correlations between moods and qualities.

Recent structuralist techniques make it possible to contrast several dimensions simultaneously; these, in turn, may bring up a considerable number of meaning and sound components, which may combine in a variety of ways. Let us consider such a "minimal pair," thought up by Richards (1929: 220) for a somewhat different purpose. One of the many sacred cows he cheerfully slaughters in *Practical Criticism* is "the notion that poetic rhythm is independent of sense."

> It is easy, however, to show how much the rhythm we *ascribe* to words (and even their inherent rhythm's sounds) is influenced by our apprehension of their meanings. Compare, for example:—
>
> Deep into a gloomy grot
>
> with
>
> Peep into a roomy cot.

"Gloomy grot" and "roomy cot" are contrasted by, roughly, such semantic features as CONFINED~SPACIOUS; ILL-LIGHTED~BROAD DAY-LIGHT; DISMAL~LIGHTSOME; SUBTERRANEAN~ON-THE-SURFACE; UN-EARTHLY~EARTHLY; GRAVE~EVERYDAY; GRAVE~LIGHT. *Deep* and *peep*

are contrasted by such semantic features as (FAR)DOWNWARD~UPWARD
("TO PEEP OVER"); GRAVE~FURTIVE; HEAVY~NIMBLE. Some of these contrasting pairs affect the rhythmic movement of these phrases (via,
perhaps, our performance), resulting in a heavy, slow cadence in the
former and a light rhythm in the latter (the heavy utterance of the
former also uses the consonant clusters /gl/ and /gr/ where in the latter
there are nonalliterative single consonants). However, in this case performance only reinforces a feeling of heaviness or lightness generated by these features. But, owing largely to the act of contrasting,
one also becomes aware in the back of one's mind of some interaction
between semantic and phonetic features. Consider the stressed long
vowels shared by the contrasted words:

-eep	into a	**oomy**	**-ot**
long		long	short
high		high	middle
bright		dark	dark

In each of the two phrases different vowel features may be used
to enhance meaning; this is the source of the double-edgedness of
the sounds. In *peep* one tends to foreground the features [BRIGHT,
HIGH], in *deep* the features [LONG, (FAR) DOWN]. In *gloomy* the feature
[DARK] whereas in *roomy* the features [LONG, HIGH] (that is, spacious)
are likely to be foregrounded. One is, indeed, tempted to quote Pope
outrageously out of context, that is, with an emphasis on *seem*:

The sound must *seem* an echo to the sense.

Sound Color

The phrase "vowel color" can be used in three different senses. The
most obvious one implies what is usually referred to as *audition colorée*,
in which each vowel is consistently associated with a specific color in the
consciousness of certain people (for an illuminating account of a rare
case of such colored hearing, see Reichard et al., 1949; see also chapter 4). The second sense refers to an association of certain oppositions
of groups of vowels with certain oppositions of abstract properties of
colors. Thus, the opposition FRONT VOWELS~BACK VOWELS is associated
with the opposition BRIGHT~DARK; and the opposition LOW~HIGH vowels is perceived as CHROMATIC~ACHROMATIC, and is associated with
MORE~LESS VARIEGATED colors. These associations of oppositions seem

to have considerable intersubjective and intercultural validity. Vowel colors in these two senses are related in the way "specific" and "general" are related. "The unambiguous tendency to feel that back vowels are 'darker' and the front vowels are 'lighter' finds further support in the assignment of darker colors to back vowels and light colors to front vowels by diverse kinds of observers" (Jakobson and Waugh, 1979: 188). At least one extremely important article (Delattre et al., 1952) uses the phrase in a third sense: the distinctive quality of each vowel as it appears to consciousness.

The first sense refers to a phenomenon whose use for poetics is not quite clear, though very interesting from the psychological point of view and fairly consistent from informant to informant (with occasional deviations). Though the notion *audition colorée* is usually invoked in discussions of Rimbaud's "Voyelles," the sonnet does not obey its rules. It associates the color "red" with the vowel /i/, for example, whereas in "genuine colored hearing" it is usually associated with /a/. We ought to look, then, for poetic significance on more abstract, less specific levels (see chapter 4). Later I shall explore the possible intersubjective basis of the association of the opposition FRONT~BACK vowels with the opposition BRIGHTNESS~DARKNESS as well as the possible relationship of the formant structure of particular sounds with other tone color qualities. During the past thirty years or so there has been an enormous breakthrough in our understanding the relationship between perceived speech sounds and the acoustic signal that carries them, but very little of this has reached literary theory and criticism. I am going to draw on some of this knowledge.

As a first approximation, I wish to point out that tone color refers, in general, to a property of sounds, the ecological value of which suggests that it may have preceded the development of language. It refers to that characteristic quality of sound, independent of pitch and loudness, from which its source or manner of production can be inferred; the quality of sound from which we infer, for instance, that what has fallen is a piece of wood or a piece of metal. The color of a sound is determined by its overtone structure. Overtones are sounds, higher in frequency than the fundamental, simultaneously emitted with it.

> But instead of this chord which should often sound quite agreeable, we usually hear a single tone, the fundamental. The others are "repressed" and replaced by the experience of tone color which

is "projected" onto the audible fundamental. . . . Without tone
color fusion we would have to analyze the complex and often
confusingly similar composition of the overtone chords, in order
to infer the substance of the sounding things and identify them.
Hence, a conscious overtone perception, if it were at all possible,
would be biologically less serviceable. (Ehrenzweig, 1965: 154)

I wish to make three comments on this description. First, the perception of overtones is impossible, in many cases, owing to physiological
limitations of the human ear. The fine discriminations it would require
exceeds the ear's capacity, and so one is able to get only a general impression of the overtone structure of the sound.[1] Second, as we shall
see in the discussion by Delattre et al. (1952), "tone color fusion" is not
a unitary process and may involve several degrees and types of fusion.
Third, Ehrenzweig's Freudian terminology of "repressing" and "pro-
jecting" ought to be supplemented by some other terminology—for
example, Polányi's.

In Polányi's terms (1967: 10–11), we might say that we have an instance of tacit knowledge, that is, of knowing more than we can tell. We
know the difference between the click of a metallic object and that of a
wooden object, but we cannot tell how we know this. We *attend from* the
proximal term, the overtone structure of the sound, *to* the distal term,
its tone color; just as in the case of human physiognomy we are attending *from* our awareness of its features *to* the characteristic appearance
of a face and thus may be unable to specify the features; or as we are
attending *from* a combination of our muscular acts *to* the performance
of a skill. "We are attending *from* these elementary movements *to* the
achievement of their purpose, and hence are unable to specify these
elementary acts. We may call this the *functional structure* of tacit know-

1. The limitations of the human ear seem to have had beneficial effects on the organism's
achievement of functional solutions. In listening to speech, people can perceive as many
as 25 or 30 phonetic segments per second; this rate would far overreach the temporal
resolving power of the ear. "Discrete acoustic events at that rate would merge into an
unanalyzable buzz," though "a listener might be able to tell from the pitch of the buzz
how fast the speaker was talking" (Liberman et al., 1967: 432). "But given that the message segments are, in fact, encoded into acoustic segments of roughly syllabic size, the
limit is set not by the number of phonetic segments per unit time but by the number of
syllables. This represents a considerable gain in the rate at which message segments can
be perceived" (Liberman et al., 1972). This elegant solution is the result of what we shall
call *parallel transmission*.

ing." Moreover, we may say that "we are aware of the proximal term of an act of tacit knowing in the appearance of its distal term." In the case of tone color, we may say that we are aware of the overtone structure of a sound in terms of the metallic click to which we are attending from it, just as we are aware of the individual features of a human physiognomy in terms of its appearance to which we are attending (or as we are aware of the several muscular moves in the exercise of a skill in the performance to which our attention is directed). This we may call the *phenomenal structure* of tacit knowing. As for the *semantic* aspect of tacit knowing, let me quote only Polányi's concluding remark on this subject: "All meaning tends to be displaced *away from ourselves*, and that is, indeed, my justification for using the terms 'proximal' and 'distal' to describe the first and second terms of tacit knowing" (ibid., 13).

At the end of an important theoretical statement of research done at the Haskins Laboratories, Liberman (1970: 321) says: "One can reasonably expect to discover whether, in developing linguistic behavior, Nature has invented new physiological devices, or simply turned old ones to new ends." The present suggestion is twofold. In some cases, at least, cognitive and physiological devices are turned to linguistic ends. This seems to reflect nature's parsimony. It is by now well established that acoustic signals for vowel perception are overtones; whereas the fundamental frequency may vary with the pitch of the speaker's voice, the vowel formant frequencies vary mainly (but not exclusively) with vowel color (in the third sense). Overtones are substantial ingredients in voiced consonants too.

Acoustic Coding

As we shall see, there is no one-to-one relationship between the segments of perceived speech and the segments of the acoustic signal that carries it. According to the Haskins theory of speech perception (for example, Liberman, 1970; Liberman et al., 1967), there is between the two a mediating step of "complex coding." The same coding can be "cued" by different acoustic signals, whereas sometimes the same acoustic signal may cue different phonemes. I have suggested that an important way by which this may be achieved can easily be described in the terms I have put forward. In production as well as in perception, we attend *from* the acoustic signal *to* the combination of muscular movements that produce it; and from these elementary movements, we attend to their joint purpose, the phoneme. The best approximation to the invariance of phonemes seems to be, according to Liberman et al. (1967: 43 and passim), by going back in the chain of articulatory events, beyond the shapes that underlie the locus of production to the *commands* that produce the shapes. At the perception end, this is frequently called the *motor theory of speech perception*.

Some poetic implications of this conception seem to be as follows: our tacit knowing of the acoustic-linguistic message, in the course of perception, seems to proceed by attending *from* the acoustic signal *to* the combination of muscular movements and, further away, to their joint purpose, the phoneme. Nonetheless, in certain circumstances, which we might call the "poetic mode," some aspects of the formant structure of the acoustic signal may vaguely enter consciousness. As a result, people may have intuitions that certain vowel contrasts correspond to BRIGHTNESS~DARKNESS, or that certain consonants sound more metallic than others. As a result, poets may more frequently use words that contain dark vowels in lines referring to dark colors, mystic obscurity, or slow and heavy movement, or in depicting hatred and struggle. At the reception end, readers may have vague intuitions that the sound patterns of these lines are somehow expressive of their atmosphere.

To spell out in detail the foregoing generalizations: Vowels consist of specific combinations of overtones, called formants. A formant is a concentration of acoustic energy within a restricted frequency region. These concentrations of energy can be converted into patches of light and shade called spectrograms, with the help of a device called a spectrograph. Three or four formants are usually seen in spectrograms of speech. In the synthetic, hand-painted spectrograms of figures 1 and 2, only the lowest two are represented. Formants are referred to by numbers as F_1, F_2, etc., the first being the lowest in frequency, the next the next higher, and so on (F_0 refers to the fundamental pitch). A formant transition is a relatively rapid change in the position of the formant on the frequency scale. A device called pattern-playback converts hand-painted spectrograms into sound. This provided the basis for what proved to be a convenient method of experimenting with the speech signal: it made it possible to vary those parameters that were guessed to be of linguistic importance and then hear the effect.

Each pattern of Figure 1 consists of two bands of acoustic energy called "formants." At the left, or beginning of each pattern the formants move rapidly through a range of frequencies. The rapid movements, which consume about 50 msec, are called "transitions." Following the transitions, the formants assume a steady state. The steady-state formants are, by their different positions on the frequency scale, the cues for the vowels /i/ and /u/. We can see that for these vowels . . . the relation between acoustic and phonetic segment is a simple, alphabetic one. There is a straight-forward correspondence in segmentation. . . . But consider now the stop consonant /d/. To isolate the acoustic cue for the segment, we should first notice the transition of the lower (first) formant. That transition is not specifically a cue for /d/; it rather tells the listener that the segment is one of the voiced stops, /b/, /d/, or /g/. . . . To produce /d/, instead of /b/, or /g/, we must add the transitions of the higher (second) formant, the parts of the pattern that are encircled by the dashed line. (Liberman, 1970: 307–8)

Now consider the following facts. If we play back only the parts of the pattern that are encircled by the dashed line, we clearly hear what we would expect to hear from the appearance of the formant transition: an upward glide in one case, and a rapidly falling whistle in the other. When the whole pattern is played back, we hear no glide or whistle, but the syllable /di/ or /du/. In figure 2 we see that the formant transition that cues /d/ is different in each context before the various vowels.

The same phoneme is cued, then, by vastly different acoustic cues.

Figure 1. Simplified spectrographic patterns sufficient to produce the syllables [di] and [du].

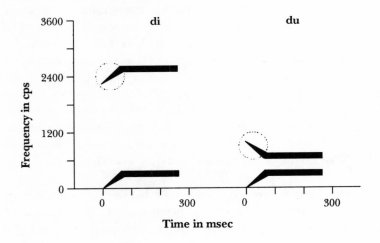

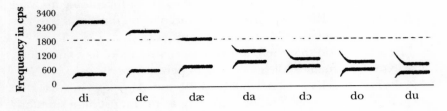

Figure 2. Spectrographic patterns sufficient for the synthesis of /d/ before vowels (dashed line at 1,800 cps shows the "locus" for /d/).

In the case of /di/, the transition rises from approximately 2,200 cps to 2,600 cps; in /du/ it falls from about 1,200 cps to 700 cps. Why do we hear these vastly different acoustic cues as the same phoneme?

Furthermore, there is no way to cut the patterns of figures 1 or 2 so as to recover /d/ segments that can be substituted for one another. We cannot cut either the /di/ or the /du/ pattern to obtain some piece that will produce /d/ alone. If we cut progressively into the syllable from the right-hand end, we hear /d/ plus a vowel, or a nonspeech sound; at no point will we hear only /d/. "This is so, because the formant transition is, at every instant, providing information about two phonemes, the consonant and the vowel—that is, the phonemes are transmitted in parallel" (Liberman et al., 1967: 436). This phenomenon is called *parallel transmission* (see note 1).

Now, parallel transmission and the fact that isolated transitions are heard as musical sound whereas the same transitions in the continuous stream of speech, even within a single nonsense syllable, is heard as speech sounds direct attention to the distinguishing marks of speech perception; they seem to indicate that we have a speech mode and a nonspeech mode of listening, which follow different paths in the neural system. We seem to be tuned, normally, to the nonspeech mode; but as soon as the incoming stream of sounds gives the slightest indication that it may be carrying linguistic information, we automatically switch to the speech mode: we attend away *from* the acoustic signal *to* the combination of muscular acts that seem to have produced it (even in the case of hand-painted spectrograms); and *from* these elementary movements *away to* their joint purpose, the phoneme sequence. "There is typically a lack of correspondence between acoustic cue and perceived phoneme, and in all these cases it appears that perception mirrors articulation more closely than sound. . . . This supports the assumption that the listener uses the inconstant sound as a basis for finding his way back to the articulatory gesture that produced it and thence, as it were, to the speaker's intent" (Liberman et al., 1967: 453).

The assumption that there are two alternative (and, to a considerable extent, mutually exclusive) modes of perception, the speech mode and the nonspeech mode, is strongly corroborated by experiments with dichotic listening (a method of delivering competing stimuli simultaneously to the two ears). There seem to be considerable differences between speech and nonspeech. "Investigators have found that speech stimuli presented to the right ear (hence, *mainly* to the left cerebral hemisphere) are better identified than those presented to the left ear (hence, *mainly* to the right cerebral hemisphere), and the reverse is true for melodies and sonar signals" (Liberman et al., 1967: 444; my italics). As will be seen in a moment, it is important to emphasize "mainly." Much crippling skepticism has sprung from an all-or-nothing conception of lateralization; and there are considerable differences, *on various linguistic levels*, between linguistic categories that cannot and that can be processed, although less efficiently, by the right hemisphere.

> A significantly greater right-ear advantage was found for the encoded stops than for the unencoded steady-state vowels.[2] The fact that the steady-state vowels are less strongly lateralized in the dominant (speech) hemisphere may be taken to mean that these sounds, being unencoded, can be, and presumably sometimes are, processed as if they were nonspeech. (ibid.; see also Jakobson and Waugh, 1979: 30–35, and Jakobson, 1980)

If right-ear (left hemisphere) advantage is characteristic of the speech mode, and left-ear (right hemisphere) advantage is characteristic of the nonspeech mode, one might reasonably speculate that the poetic mode of speech perception is characterized by some way of overcoming this channel separation or specialization. Certain perceptual qualities characteristic of a certain acoustic signal when processed in the nonspeech mode (mainly by the right hemisphere) are eliminated from consciousness when the same signal is processed in the speech mode (mainly by the left hemisphere). In the poetic mode, some

2. The authors use the terms "encoded" and "unencoded" to indicate whether the perception of a phoneme does or does not require restructuring during the conversions from the acoustic signal to the phoneme. Unencodedness is relative, because *all* speech sounds require a considerable amount of restructuring.

nonspeech qualities of the signal seem to become accessible, however faintly, to consciousness.

One might reasonably speculate whether the processing of a signal in the speech mode does or does not entail its parallel processing in the nonspeech mode. In other words, the question is whether the acoustic signal is shut out from the nonspeech processor once it enters the speech processor, or is the *output* of the nonspeech processor shut out from consciousness once the output of the speech processor is attended to? My speculations are more consistent with the latter possibility. There is, indeed, some experimental evidence that supports me. Liberman et al. describe an experiment by T. Rand:

> To one ear he presented all the first formant, including the transitions, together with the steady-state parts of the second and third formants; when presented alone, these patterns sound vaguely like /da/. To the other ear, with proper time relationships carefully preserved, were presented the 50-msec second-formant and third-formant transitions; alone, these sound like ... chirps. ... But when these patterns were presented together—that is, dichotically—listeners clearly heard /ba/, /da/ or /ga/ (depending on the nature of the second-formant and third-formant transitions) in one ear and, simultaneously, nonspeech chirps in the other. Thus, it appears that the same acoustic events—the second-formant or third-formant transitions—can be processed simultaneously as speech and nonspeech. We should suppose, then, that the incoming signal goes indiscriminately to speech and nonspeech processors. If the speech processors succeed in extracting phonetic features, then the signal is speech; if they fail, the signal is processed only as nonspeech. [see also Rakerd et al., 1981; Liberman and Isenberg, 1980; Repp, 1984; Repp et al., 1983]

I have arrived at the notion of the poetic mode on the basis of introspection and the thought-experiments reported below. However, I received massive corroboration that nonphonetic acoustic information may be available in the speech mode too when Repp's comprehensive survey of research on categorical perception was published in 1984. Thus, for instance, "Liberman et al. (1957) were able to generate a fair prediction of discrimination performance from known labeling probabilities; however, performance was somewhat better than predicted, suggesting that the subjects did have some additional stimulus information available" (245).

What is more, people appear to be capable of switching modes by using different listening strategies. Fricative stimuli seem to be especially suited for the application of different strategies so that they may be perceived fairly categorically in one situation but continuously in another (ibid., 287). Repp has investigated the possibility that with fricatives, for instance, little training would be necessary for acoustic discrimination of within-category differences. He employed an /s/-/š/ continuum, followed by a vocalic context. The success of his procedure

> together with the introspections of the experienced listeners, suggested that the skill involved lay in perceptually segregating the noise from its vocalic context, which then made it possible to attend to its "pitch." Without this segregation, the phonetic percept was dominant. Once the auditory strategy has been acquired, it is possible to switch back and forth between auditory and phonetic modes of listening, and it seems likely . . . that both strategies could be pursued simultaneously (or in very rapid succession) without any loss of accuracy. These results provide good evidence for the existence of two alternative modes of perception, phonetic and auditory—a distinction supported by much additional evidence. (307)

It is reassuring to find that my speculations gain support from an increasing body of experimental evidence and that cognitive strategies have been discovered by which listeners may switch, at will, back and forth between phonetic categories and auditory information. Although once in the auditory mode "it is possible either to selectively attend to individual auditory dimensions or to divide attention between several of them" (ibid., 307), Repp's "auditory mode" does not abolish the distinction between the speech and nonspeech modes. It merely provides evidence that even in the speech mode *some* precategorical sensory information is accessible, that is, that the poetic mode *is* possible.

Thought-Experiment with "Metallic" Consonants

To illuminate the relationship between the speech mode, the nonspeech mode, and the poetic mode, let us perform a thought-experiment based on some real experimental findings by Liberman and his colleagues. I have presented to some of my friends and colleagues the following question: "Which sound is more metallic, /b/ or /g/?" It is interesting to note that none of these people claimed for a moment that they did not know what I was talking about (if this question arose at all, it was not before my informants answered my question with considerable confidence). In other words, my informants readily entered the poetic mode. But, more significantly, without exception they had no doubt that /g/ was the more metallic sound of the two. They exhibited less confidence when they were asked to place /d/ on this continuum. Though confident that it was less metallic than /g/, some of my informants were not sure enough whether it was more or less metallic than /b/. However, a fairly consistent pattern eventually emerged: the continuum /b/, /d/, /g/, in an ascending order of metallicness. Can we account for this perceptual difference between these three voiced stops? One thing is certain: None of the places of articulation of these consonants is more metallic than of the others.

We have, then, some fairly unanimous intuitions that the consonants /b, d, g/ constitute a sequence of increasing metallicness. If we are to make sense of these intuitions, we have to proceed in three stages. First, we must try to find out in what if any verifiable respect these consonants constitute an increasing scale? Second, we must assume that this scale is analogous to the scale of metallicness. Third, we must find reasons for matching precisely the /g/ extreme of the consonant sequence with the metallic extreme of the corresponding continuum. Though they appear to be unique and discrete linguistic events, can one place the /b, d, g/ continuum on a more/less continuum of any of their acoustic or phonetic properties? To explore a possible answer, we turn to another set of classical experiments conducted at the Haskins Laboratories.

Categorical perception is one of the most important characteristics of the speech mode. It was explored at Haskins and the findings published. To save space, I quote a brief summary by Glucksberg and Danks (1975: 40–41) of two of the articles (Liberman et al., 1957; Mattingly et al., 1971).

> Although the physical stimuli may vary continuously over a fairly wide range, we do not perceive this variation. Consider the continuous series of changes in the second formant of a simple English syllable, shown in figure 3. These sound patterns produce the syllables /ba/, /da/ and /ga/ when fed into a speech synthesizer. The first three syllables are heard as /ba/, the next six as /da/, and the last five as /ga/. . . . The three /b/'s all sound the same, even though there is continuous change along a single dimension. Be-

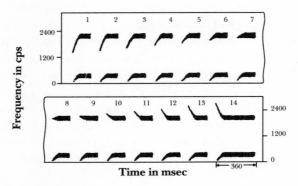

Figure 3. Illustrations of the spectrographic patterns from which the stimuli of the experiment were made.

tween stimuli 3 and 4, listeners perceive a shift from /b/ to /d/. This difference is always perceived as quite distinct, even though it is physically no more different than the difference between stimuli 2 and 3 or between 4 and 5. The phenomenon of poor discrimination within categories and excellent discrimination across categories is known as *categorical perception*. . . . If only the first bit of the second formant is played on a speech synthesizer, we no longer hear the sound as speech, and we then hear equally discriminable chirps along the whole range.

It is fascinating to listen to these synthesized sound series. Through repeated listening to a demo tape of speech synthesis by Terry Halwes, the question about the relative metallicness of /b/ and /g/ was suggested to me. Listening to the /ba/, /da/, /ga/ series and to the series of excised formant transitions has the effect of a shock on the innocent listener. When listening to the ascending series of second-formant transitions on more than usually sensitive equipment, some listeners seemed to be confused. At the beginning of the sequence they felt it was a gradually rising series; at some point toward the end they felt that the tone color rather than the pitch was gradually changing. Let us review the stimuli in light of these perceptions. The second-formant transition of stimulus 1 is a long, upward glide in an extremely short time. It covers a span of 840 cps (that is, in this range, about two-thirds of an octave) in 50 msec. This exceeds the resolving power of the human ear so that only a short section of the glide is consciously perceived;

the rest of it is fused in a way not unlike overtone fusion, yielding a tone color that is not the same in all the stimuli of the series. Where the glides are long enough, there is a gradual change in the perceived pitch from stimulus to stimulus, even though their target frequency is the same. The perceived pitch of the chirp seems to be determined by a weighted average of the series of frequencies covered. Since the target frequency is the same in all stimuli, the shorter the second-formant transition, the higher the average. Around stimuli 6–10, the perceived pitch does not seem to change very much; the gradual change of the transition frequencies is fused into the target pitch and is perceived as a gradual change of tone color. The second-formant transition of the last stimulus in this series is a swift downward glide of considerable length (720 cps) to the same target frequency.

Now notice this: the first glide rises from a point of 1,320 cps to 2,160 cps, whereas the last one falls from a point of 2,880 cps to the same target frequency. The difference between these two onset frequencies is 1,560 cps, which in this frequency range means well over one octave. Such a span allows for considerable variation in the perceived pitches of the chirps as well as for considerable variation in their tone color (caused by tone fusion). The higher the fused tones, the greater the sharpness and brilliance they impute on the chirps; hence, their relative metallicness. We must assume, then, that *some* of this relative sharpness and brilliance of the acoustic signal of /g/, at least, may become accessible to consciousness in the speech mode—even though it is a stop, that is, one of the most highly encoded speech sounds (the special process that decodes the stops is said to strip away all sensory information from the acoustic signal).[3]

This thought-experiment may help us explain one of Hrushovski's interesting examples of onomatopoeia from Hebrew poetry: "The word *šrika* [whistle] is onomatopoeia; however, in Alterman's phrase *šrikat hakatarim* a new onomatopoeia is created: to the 'whistling' sound the repetition of the group **kat-kat** is added; this sound . . . reminds the reader of a new meaning that is not explicitly mentioned in the text:

3. We are concerned here with a frequency range that is fairly high. The human ear has added sensitivity to this region, although it is well above the fundamental frequencies of the human voice and most musical instruments. The onset frequency of stimulus 14 is one or two tones higher than the highest tones of the violin, a full octave higher than the highest tones of the soprano, three octaves higher than the highest tones of the tenor, and so forth.

the sound of the rushing wheels of the train." He quotes a similar instance of sound patterns imitating the sound of the rushing train from the Hebrew poet Shlonsky (1968: 414). As for the sound patterns /ta/ and /k+t/, the relevant consonants are voiceless plosives that are cued by abrupt, nonperiodic noises; in this respect, these sound patterns are analogous to the sound of the rushing wheels. But /p/ too is a voiceless plosive. Why do both Shlonsky and Alterman use /kat-kat/ rather than, say, /pat-pat/ for sound imitation? Why does the clock say tick-tock or the like in many languages rather than, say, pit-pot? The reason is to be sought in the relative metallicness of the phonemes. The sequence /p, t, k/ is the voiceless analogue of the sequence /b, d, g/; and /p/ is the least metallic phoneme of the sequence. Language cannot give an exact imitation of the noises of nature. While natural noises are of an infinite variety, and their perception is continuous rather than categorical, the linguistic sounds imitating them are limited to about thirty phonetic categories perceived categorically. Consequently, the resemblance of the phoneme combinations to the imitated natural noises is necessarily poor; at most, one speaks of certain aspects of certain groups of phonemes that are *more or less* analogous to certain outstanding properties of the noises: voiceless plosives are more abrupt than other speech sounds, and the plosives /k+t/ are more metallic than /p+t/, and as such are perceived as analogous to the metallic abrupt sounds of running wheels.[4]

When the acoustic signal is processed in the nonspeech mode (by the right hemisphere of the brain), we hear it as if we heard music sounds or natural noises. We attend away from overtone structure to tone color. When the same signal is processed in the speech mode (by the left cerebral hemisphere), this tone color is suppressed. We attend away from formant structure to phoneme. In the poetic mode, the main processing is identical with the processing in the speech mode. However, some tone color from the processing in the nonspeech mode faintly enters consciousness.

I cannot consider here the question whether the poetic mode is a submode of the speech mode, or a mode in its own right. Perhaps the question is similar to whether the zebra has white stripes on a black ground or black stripes on a white ground.

---

4. For a possible supplementary explanation, see note 3 in chapter 5.

A Digression on Figurative Language

If I am justified in my speculations on the nature of the poetic mode, and if Liberman (1970: 320) is right in his suggestion that our understanding of the significance of the differences between the more and less deeply encoded aspects of the system "may, in turn, give us insight into analogous differences at the higher levels," we should not be surprised if we find that these characteristics are not confined to the level of speech perception. There are, indeed, some findings at the level of figurative language that indicate this possibility. I have elsewhere elaborated on these issues (Tsur, 1987: 145–90; also Tsur, 1992, chapter 8); here I wish to draw attention to a curious finding that must be relevant. There seems to be some evidence that abstract nouns are double-edged in an interesting way. In some contexts they are *the* vehicle of highly differentiated conceptual thinking; in others they may be the vehicle of some lowly differentiated, emotionally loaded atmosphere. One typical condition in which this may be the case relates to the use of abstract nouns in the description of a specific, concrete landscape (as in the octets of Wordsworth's Dover Beach sonnet and Westminster Bridge sonnet or of Baudelaire's "Recueillement"). It also should be noticed that in several cultures emotionally loaded exclamations are intimately related to the pathetic fallacy, that is, to the bestowal of the speaker's feelings on surrounding nature.

Considering that such global activities as emotions and spatial orientation are intimately associated with the right hemisphere, one might surmise that in poetic and rhetorical practice spatial orientation may be a preferred instrument to transfer part of the processing of the verbal message to the right hemisphere. This idea could be elaborated in the following way. At least two kinds of information about semantic categories are stored in memory: not only *names* of categories, but representations of their *properties*. In the course of normal speech (that is, in the speech mode), we perceive the representations of these properties categorically; we do not perceive semantic features (or meaning components), but a single, compact semantic entity that they constitute. When a landscape description (in the world stratum of the poem) and certain stylistic devices (such as repetitive schemata both on the semantic and phonetic levels) activate the right hemisphere (or, alternatively, transfer a significant part of the processing of the message to the right hemisphere), representations of some or many properties of these categories escape the control of categorical perception and constitute some global and diffuse atmosphere in a concrete landscape.

Thought-Experiment with "Dark" Vowels

Let us turn to a second thought-experiment, based on another set of real experiments at the Haskins Laboratories back in the early fifties, that offers an explanation for our intuition that back vowels are darker than front vowels. Certain physical qualities of the acoustic signal enter consciousness, in spite of the speech mode, when we perceive back vowels as dark and front vowels as bright. These associations seem to have general, culture-independent validity. The search for an explanation is summarized by Jakobson and Waugh (1979: 188–94).

I submit, in accordance with the structuralist conception, that it is more adequate to conceive of the back-front continuum as analogous in some way to the dark-light continuum than to attribute specific properties to the individual vowels. To this effect, Jakobson and Waugh (ibid., 189) quote Gombrich with approval:

> The problem of synaesthetic equivalences will cease to look embarrassingly arbitrary if, hereto, we fix our attention not on likeness of elements but on structural relationships within a scale or a matrix. When we say that *i* is brighter than *u*, we find a surprising degree of general consent. If we are more careful still and say that the step from *u* to *i* is more like an upward step than a downward step, I think the majority will agree, whatever explanation each of us may be inclined to offer.

In other words, there need not be anything inherently dark in the vowel /u/, or inherently bright in the vowel /i/. Suffice that the vowel continuum and the brightness continuum are perceived as somehow analogous to one another, and that the vowel /u/ and the value dark occupy similar positions on them. However, we still have to explain why the bright end of the brightness continuum is matched precisely with the front extreme of the vowel continuum and not the other way around; or, likewise, why the high end of the height continuum is matched with the /i/ end of the vowel continuum rather than the other way around. My claim is, again, that certain perceptual aspects of the acoustic signal, irrelevant in principle to the speech mode, do enter consciousness in spite of all. Consider the widespread intuition expressed by Gombrich that the step from /u/ to /i/ is more upward than downward. In an important sense, each vowel can be uttered on any fundamental pitch. Yet in another, no less important, sense the two vowels are exactly the same height. This will be apparent if we look again at figure 2. The first formants of the two vowels are of exactly the same frequency (250 cps). If, on the other hand, we look at the frequency of the second formants, we find that the one for /i/ is of a much higher frequency than the one for /u/ (2,900 vs. 700 cps; for the numbers, see Delattre et al., 1952: 198). It should be noted that this intuition of an upward step from /u/ to /i/ can easily be overridden when the fundamental pitch pattern goes in the opposite direction, as in *intrude*!

Now, what about the correspondence of the dark-bright continuum to the /u/-/i/ continuum? Let us grant that these continua should be made analogous. Why should the /i/ pole be matched precisely with the bright pole and not the other way around? In what acoustic features relevant to the opposition DARK~BRIGHT are the back vowels opposed to the front vowels? Looking at figure 2, we might say that the significantly higher second formant bestows some luster on the front vowels. This assumption is corroborated by the effects of reducing the intensity of the higher formant of most front vowels and some middle vowels. "Small attenuations of the higher formant caused the vowel to acquire a quality that can best be described as 'dull'" (Delattre et al., 1952: 204).

But a much more interesting side to the story emerges, having considerable psychological consequences. In figure 2 the three rightmost spectrograms are of back vowels, the three leftmost of front vowels. In the former, the two formants are significantly closer to one another than in the latter. Figure 4 shows, though in a less transparent manner, that the same kind of correlation is true of all sixteen cardinal vowels of the IPA. Delattre and his colleagues produced good experimental evidence that vowels whose first and second formants are closer together are perceived differently from those whose formants are wider apart. Roughly, the human ear effectively fuses the two formants when they are close enough to one another, whereas it seems to perceive them as fairly differentiated when they are sufficiently apart. In an important sense, the formant structure of the front vowels is more clearly articulated. Alternatively, one might say that the ear averages the first and second formant frequencies of the back vowels, whereas the first two formants of the front vowels, though perceived categorically, clearly stand out in our subliminal perception. For the vowels where the first

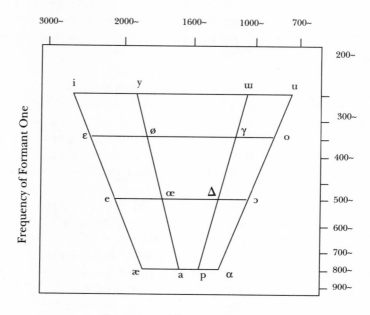

Figure 4. The acoustic location of the synthetic vowels, plotted according to the frequency positions of the first and second formants.

two formants are relatively close together, one can find reasonably good one-formant equivalents that occupy an intermediate position between the two-formant vowels (nearer to the lower formant). It is difficult to find one-formant equivalents for the front vowels in which the two formants are rather far apart, except for /i/, which has the greatest separation of the first and second formants; here, a single formant near the normal position of the *second* formant seems to produce the /i/ color rather well. "/i/ is an extreme vowel (none has a higher second formant), and the kind of judgment-anchoring which so often occurs at the extremes of a stimulus series might account for the fact that a high-frequency formant was so often identified as /i/" (Delattre et al., 205).

In other words, the two formants of the front vowels stand so clearly apart that they cannot be averaged. In the case of /i/, the one-formant version is *not* a result of averaging but is due to the fact that the high second formant can cue no other vowel. The ear may seize on it without going into further niceties. There is, then, a continuum of decreasing effort required for processing the various vowels. This continuum can be parsed into three clear stages: first, in back vowels, perceiving a fused acoustic signal and reanalyzing its formant frequency into its constituent formants; second, in front vowels, perceiving and discriminating two well-articulated formants; third, with /i/, perceiving a single formant without further discrimination. This assumption is corroborated by the effect of reducing the intensity of the lower formant of the back vowels, which caused a change in color toward the adjacent vowel. "We should suppose, then, that reducing the intensity of the lower formant . . . would have the effect of increasing the higher formant's relative contribution to the 'mean' and would thus effectively raise the mean formant" (ibid., 203). When, however, the lower formant's intensity was reduced in the front vowels, "the vowel color was replaced by a nonvowel sound. . . . In no case did a reduction in the intensity of the lower formant cause a clear *shift* in vowel color" (ibid.).

It is worth noting that the perception of *both* front and back vowels is subject to what the Haskins investigators came to call "categorical perception" so characteristic of the speech mode. The difference is that the system more easily exits speech mode (and categorical perception) where front vowels are concerned. Where nonspeech sounds are concerned, no categorical perception and no averaging take place. With arbitrarily chosen two-formant patterns, which did not sound like vowels, "the two formants of the nonvowel pattern, however close together they may be, did not fuse into a single sound, but tended rather to be heard as two-component chords" (206).

We might conclude, then, that in the case of the fused formants of the back vowels, as well as in the averaged one-formant versions, the ear reanalyzes a lowly differentiated acoustic signal in terms of the frequencies that appear to have been fused in it. This may be the application, at a lower level, of a mechanism underlying the motor theory of speech perception mentioned earlier.

How does this bear on the analogy of the vowel continuum with the brightness continuum? The acoustic signal of the back vowels is of relatively low differentiation. The impression from two formants received by the ear is sufficiently indistinguishable from that of one formant to place it somewhere intermediate between them. I submit, then, that relatively low differentiation and relative darkness are similar phenomenally to a sufficient degree to warrant matching the back vowel extreme of the vowel continuum with the dark extreme of the brightness continuum. Some perceptual quality of the acoustic signal sometimes intrudes into the speech mode, creating the poetic mode.

A still further step is required to complete our thought-experiment. Relatively low differentiation in vowel perception is naturally matched with darkness when the two continua are perceived as analogous. When back vowels are frequent in verse lines that refer to dark colors, the dark potential of the vowels is realized by combination with the dark elements of the meaning. Readers may intuit that the sound is somehow "an echo of the sense," or that the sounds are somehow "expressive" of the sense. It would appear that the conventionally established metaphorical relationship between darkness and mystic obscurity, or such emotions as hatred, is mediating between vowel color and such meaning components. I wish to suggest, however, that the relatively undifferentiated perceptions associated with the back vowels may be *directly related to* the lowly differentiated perception associated with mystic obscurities, and there is no need for a mediating metaphorical concept. Likewise, in light of my analysis of emotions and emotional qualities elsewhere (Tsur, 1978), low differentiation is a characteristic of emotional (as opposed to rational) qualities. Combined with high energy level, it can be an important ingredient in such emotions and emotional qualities as anger or hatred. Thus, when back vowels are frequent in verse lines depicting hatred or struggle, they may be perceived as expressive, with no need, again, for a mediating metaphorical concept. The foregoing analysis of the structural relationship between back vowels, darkness, mystic obscurity, and hatred or struggle may be regarded as further reinforcing one of the basic tenets of this study: that "past experience" insufficiently explains certain metaphorical intuitions; that some metaphorical relationships originate in processes that are deeper than cultural conditioning; and that certain culturally conditioned metaphorical conventions are results rather than causes, and they came to reflect, through repeated cultural transmission, certain underlying cognitive processes.

I have introduced the article by Delattre and his collaborators (1952) to account for the ubiquitous intuition that back vowels are darker than front vowels. That introduction also could serve as a basis for explaining the positive correlation of back vowels with mystic obscurity and hatred or struggle in poetry. In the next section I shall attempt with its help to explain some additional correlations.

In my book on metrics I have applied to metrical theory the cognitive principle that in a sequence of two coordinate items, other things being equal, it is more natural for the longer one to come last; it involves a lesser burden on the perceiver's short-term memory (Tsur, 1977: 76). The same principle applies to idiomatic phrases, such as "high and mighty" rather then "mighty and high," "bed and breakfast" rather than "breakfast and bed," "part and parcel," "blood and thunder," etc. In an important sense, relatively dark vowels seem to be marked in a way that renders them equivalent to relatively long words. Thus, we have phrases of two coordinate words, the second of which contains a prominent syllable that is darker than the prominent syllable of the first word; for instance: "sweet and sour," "flesh and blood," "safe and sound," "high and low," "meek and mild," "tit for tat," even "Peter and Paul" (overriding relative length), and "back and forth" (overriding logical order). Likewise, we have a long list of varied reduplications, going from the lighter to the darker vowel rather than from darker to lighter: "seesaw," "Ping-Pong," "sing-song," "ding-dong," "chit-chat," "tip-top," etc. Phrases like "sick and tired," "bread and butter," "milk and water" use both modes of marking, and so does "milk and honey," even though the order of words has been determined in Hebrew. This is, of course, only a tendency, not a foolproof rule.

There seems, then, to be some sort of equivalence between word length and phonetic darkness, determined by their greater load on the cognitive apparatus. Our cognitive economy tends to relegate to the end of the phrase (or clause) anything that requires relatively great processing effort, whether owing to relative word length or the relative difficulty of discriminating between the formants that constitute the back vowel's acoustic signal. In this sense, back vowels occupy more mental processing space and are perceived as heavier, or slower, or, at any rate, relatively marked. This can offer one possible explanation for the relative frequency of dark vowels in verse lines referring to slow and heavy movements. I shall return to this issue at the end of chapter 2.

A Real Experiment

It has been suggested that we might conduct a "real" experiment[5] to find out whether subjects who perceive back vowels as darker than

---

5. This part of the research was jointly conducted with Yehosheba Bentov, Ruth Lavy, and Hanna Lock.

front vowels do indeed also perceive them as more complicated. So, we have conducted an experiment in which subjects were requested to characterize /u/ and /i/ with four pairs of antonymous adjectives directly applicable to the precategorical sensory information.

Subjects. Subjects were 120 students at the Seminar Hakkibbutsim teachers' training college, who were asked by their teacher to stay after the lesson, to take an experimental test.

Stimuli. The test material consisted of a sheet with the vowels /i/ and /u/ (in two conditions) printed in Hebrew and a list of eight pairs of antonymous adjectives. The test was forced-choice: subjects were requested to characterize each vowel by the more suitable member of each pair. In one condition the vowels were printed in isolation, in the other as part of the nonsense syllables /pit/ and /put/ (the word *pitput* means "chatter" in Hebrew). The test was administered to sixty subjects in each condition. Initially, the two conditions were meant to constitute a pilot test to choose the one that would yield more significant results. As will be seen, the differences between the two conditions were insignificant; however, the *direction* and *consistency* of the differences were rather significant. Two groups of pairs of adjectives were used. Four pairs (DARK~BRIGHT, FAR~NEAR, BIG~SMALL, LOW~HIGH) refer to perceived qualities regularly and quite consistently associated with these vowels. Four pairs (THICK~THIN, DIFFERENTIATED~UNDIFFERENTIATED, SPACIOUS~DENSE, SIMPLE~COMPLICATED) were the test adjectives and were chosen because they may characterize the perceived quality of the acoustic information as discussed. This structure was chosen mainly to get around a problem of communication with the subjects. If you explain to them clearly what kind of intuition you are looking for, you may interfere with their spontaneous response; and if you refrain from such an explanation, you cannot be sufficiently sure that the responses reflect the *kind* of perceived qualities you are interested in. For this reason the first four pairs of adjectives were included. They could, on the one hand, specify to some extent the kind of task the subjects were expected to perform on the test items; on the other, they could indicate whether the subjects understood the task.

Four pairs of adjectives also were included in the second group, not for symmetry, but because of the uncertainty concerning which pair would describe the perceived quality of the acoustic information least ambiguously. The possibility of such an ambiguity has been confirmed, unexpectedly enough, in relation to one pair of adjectives in the first group (see below). In this respect, the present test was initially intended as a pilot to choose the appropriate pair of adjectives. The results, however, were surprisingly unambiguous (in the expected direction) with respect to all four test pairs.

A few comments on the adjective pairs used. The Hebrew adjectives for THICK~THIN do not have the ambiguity of the English adjectives. *Samikh* means "thick" as in the phrases "thick syrup" and "thick smoke"; *dalil* (meaning "sparse" or "diluted") is perceived as its proper antonym. *Meruwah* in the third pair is ambiguous, meaning "spacious" or "wide open"; so there was a danger that it might be referred to the articulatory gesture rather than to the acoustic correlates, but its antonym means clearly "dense, crowded, compact." There was a suspicion that the expected use of DIFFERENTIATED~UNDIFFERENTIATED might be unfamiliar to the subjects. Finally, the adjectives SIMPLE~COMPLICATED are too abstract, and so it might be doubtful whether the subjects applied them to the sensory qualities of the acoustic correlates of the vowels or to some other aspects. Thus, it was expected that the adjectives THICK~THIN should best reflect the subjects' intuitions concerning the vowel's sensory qualities. The results are given in table 1.

All pairs of adjectives except one were very significantly attributed more frequently in the expected way than the other way around. The only pair that showed a tendency opposite to expectation was HIGH~LOW. This seems rather odd, since the intuition that the step from /u/ to /i/ is more upward than downward is fairly consistent. Two factors seem to have influenced these deviant results. First, the results drew attention to the fact that the relevant Hebrew adjectives are ambiguous, meaning either HIGH~LOW or TALL~SHORT. Second, the occurrence of this adjective pair after the pairs BIG~SMALL and FAR~NEAR may have influenced subjects to construe it as referring to relative size rather than relative pitch.

When we compare the results for the /i/~/u/ pair with the results for the /pit/~/put/ pair, we find exactly the same general tendency, as well as similar numbers for each particular pair; the dominant attribution is only insignificantly lower for /pit/~/put/, whereas the recessive attribution is correspondingly higher. The relation between the two curves can be seen in figure 5.

Such results can be explained in terms of Rakerd's (1984) finding that "vowels in consonantal context are more linguistically perceived than are isolated vowels." In other words, the perception of vowels in consonantal context is more categorical, whereas in isolated vowels more precategorical information can be perceived; alternatively, the sensory information underlying a vowel, by virtue of which it is typically associated with certain perceptual qualities, varies from one consonantal context to another, owing to "parallel transmission," that is, owing to "the fact that a talker often co-articulates the neighboring segments of an utterance (that is, overlaps their respective productions) such that the acoustic signal is jointly influenced by those segments" (123).

We have been seeking experimental support for certain speculations in cognitive poetics, namely, (1) in many cases the perceptual qualities associated with certain speech sounds can be accounted for by assuming that in the poetic mode *some* of the rich precategorical sensory information underlying the speech sound does reach consciousness; and (2) the perception of rounded back vowels as darker than the unrounded front vowels can be accounted for by the fact that F_1 and F_2 of back vowels are less differentiated, closer together, than those of front

Table 1. The majority of subjects characterizes /i/ as "lighter, nearer, smaller, thinner, more differentiated, more spacious and simpler" than /u/.

phoneme	dark	light	n.r.	far	near	n.r.	big	small	n.r.	low	high	n.r.
/i/	6	53	1	14	45	1	6	51	3	33	25	2
/pit/	14	46	—	20	40	—	17	43	—	36	23	1
/u/	53	6	1	46	14	—	52	7	1	26	31	3
/put/	46	14	—	40	20	—	43	17	—	23	36	1

phoneme	thick	thin	n.r.	undif.	dif.	n.r.	dense	spac.	n.r.	simp.	comp.	n.r.
/i/	9	49	2	21	37	2	18	39	3	51	8	1
/pit/	13	47	—	26	33	1	25	35	—	50	9	1
/u/	50	9	1	37	22	1	39	19	2	8	51	1
/put/	47	13	—	33	26	1	35	25	—	9	50	1

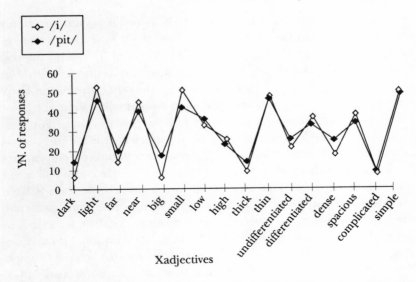

Figure 5. Notice that in the *pit* curve the peaks and ebbs are consistently nearer to one another than in the *i* curve.

vowels. Our findings have been thoroughly consistent with these hypotheses. It is, however, questionable whether they constitute sufficient proof for them. Consequently, the validity of our "proof" crucially depends on the extent to which our findings fit with related facts and findings.

Angry and Tender Consonants

With the foregoing explanation in mind, let us return to Fónagy's data concerning the distribution of consonants in tender and angry poems. As was noted, the majority of consonants occur about equally in both groups of poems. I was wondering whether in some cases at least this equal distribution could not be attributed to the double-edgedness of certain sounds, that is, to the conflicting aspects of their combinational potential that cancel out each other's effects on statistics. There seems to be, indeed, some faint evidence to such mutual cancellation. The mean value of the frequency of /g/ in the tender poems of Hugo and Verlaine is 1.30 percent; in their aggressive poems it was 1.21 percent, an insignificant difference, indeed. However, the individual numbers for the two poets seem to be rather significant. /g/ occurs over one and a half times more frequently in Verlaine's tender poems than in his angry ones (1.63: 1.07), whereas we find almost the reverse proportion in Hugo's poems: 0.96 percent in his tender poems, and 1.35 percent in his angry ones. Likewise, the frequency of /d/ in the tender poems of the two poets is 7.51 percent, whereas in their angry poems it is 7.94 percent. But taken individually, again, the same sound has opposite emotional tendencies for the two poets. For Verlaine, its quality is basically tender (10.11:7.93), whereas for Hugo it has a basically aggressive quality (7.09:5.76). For Petőfi, both consonants are insignificantly more tender than angry. There are two possible explanations for these data. According to the first, these sounds have no emotional potentials of their own: the various poets may associate them in an arbitrary manner with any emotional quality, according to their idiosyncrasies. As these sounds recur, an emotional quality accrues to them according to their emotional contexts in each poet's work. The second explanation assumes that from the various acoustic, phonetic, and phonological features certain elements of the combinational potential may be abstracted, some of which may be conflicting.

It is difficult to give direct reasons for preferring any of these explanations, except that the second is more consistent with my analysis. This in itself is a not too strong reason that can be reinforced by a rewriting exercise performed by Hrushovski (1980: 44):

> Now, if this is the case, would not any sound pattern do? Let us try to "rewrite" the Shakespearean lines using words similar in content:
>
> > When to the crux of crucial quiet thought
> > I crave and call remembrance of things past[.]
>
> We have already created a very similar network of sounds, this time based on the repetition of *K*, strengthened by the cluster *K* + *R* (involving the original word "remembrance" too). Nevertheless, it seems that this sound pattern cannot possibly express silence, though "quiet thought" starts with *K* as "silent thought" starts with *S*. It is plausible that a reader will impute to this text something strong and harsh, reinforced by the sound pattern. The pivotal word may become "crux," though its counterpart "sessions" was subordinated to "sweet silent thought." One may generalize that, in a part of a text in which a sound pattern coexists with a number

of semantic elements, the sound pattern may contribute to shifting the center of gravity from one direction of meaning to another.

Had the speech sounds no expressive potential of their own, the network of sounds based on /k/ would have readily assumed the emotional quality of quietness, which it does not. Here the sound tends to confer on the text "something strong and harsh" and "may contribute to shifting the center of gravity from one direction of meaning to another" (for example, from *quiet* to *crux*). However, this putative shifting of the center of gravity became possible only through a regularization of meter in the transcription: the two successive, alliterating stressed syllables in "sweet silent" foreground these words and focus attention on their meanings. So let us amend the transcription to

When to the quorum of kind, quiet thought

also reinstating some of the legal connotations of the original text. But notice this: even though we are now prevented from shifting the center of gravity to some other "pivotal word," the /k/ sound retains its hard and strong quality and by no means becomes expressive of some "kind, quiet" atmosphere originating in the meaning of the words. The sound pattern becomes either neutral or improper to the emotion expressed. As this exercise may testify, speech sounds do have emotional potential of their own, and one may not ascribe to them just any quality suggested by the text's meaning.

Now, why is /k/ so hard and its repeated occurrence incompatible with an atmosphere of silence? And why are the voiced stops /d, g/ double-edged? If we relate these voiced stops to their voiceless counterparts /t, k/ that were positively correlated with aggression, and to the sonorants /l, m/ that were negatively correlated, we find that /d, g/ resemble the first group in one respect and the second group in another. As a preliminary, let us quote Fry's concise account (1970: 35–36):

> The ear and the brain are quick to seize upon the difference between periodic and aperiodic sounds, between tones and noises, and can detect within very close limits the moment at which periodicity begins. In normal speech, all vowel sound, semi-vowels, liquids and nasals are periodic sounds, while noiseless consonants are aperiodic. Between these two classes, there are the voiced fricatives in which the ear recognizes an underlying periodicity, even though it is accompanied by aperiodic friction noise. In distin-

guishing between voiced and voiceless plosives, the exact moment at which periodicity begins is among the cues used by the listener.

Thus, the sequence vowels, liquids, and nasals, voiced fricatives, voiced stops, voiceless fricatives, voiceless stops, constitute a scale of decreasing periodicity or sonority, in this order. The feature [±PERI-ODIC] is responsible for the opposition TONES~NOISES, which is analogous, in a sense, to the opposition HARMONIOUS~NOT HARMONIOUS, or SOFT~HARD. There are two more relevant oppositions in the scale: CONTINUOUS~ABRUPT, and ENCODED~UNENCODED. The latter is *a scale of relative encodedness* rather than a dichotomy, and one should bear in mind that even the least encoded speech sounds are very much encoded. The optimal tender sounds are periodic (voiced), continuous, and relatively unencoded; the optimal aggressive sounds are aperiodic (voiceless), abrupt, and highly encoded. Now it should be emphasized that two points (or even two areas) on this scale can be picked out and presented in opposition to each other as more or less aggressive; liquids and nasals are not inherently tender, and voiceless stops are not inherently aggressive. When we see in Fónagy's table (197) that a sound like /d/ or /g/ is aggressive for one poet and tender for another, even in the same language, this may suggest that Verlaine treated /d/ as an abrupt and encoded sound and opposed it to continuous and relatively unencoded sounds, subduing its voiced feature; whereas in /g/ he subdued the abrupt and encoded features and opposed it to /k/ along the [±VOICED] feature. Hugo did just the reverse. We must grant the poets a considerable degree of free choice *within the constraints* of the sounds' combinational potential. Hence, the double-edged nature of these sounds.

The order of items on the scale is not unambiguous, precisely because the features vary independently. I have ordered the items according to the periodicity feature. According to the continuity and encodedness features, voiceless fricatives ought to have preceded voiced stops. Since, however, what matters is that owing to these conflicting features the sounds are double-edged, and can be separately contrasted to the other sounds on each of these features, their exact order in the middle of the scale seems insignificant. It should be noted that /r/, although a periodic liquid, has outstanding aggressive potentials, especially in languages in which it is rolled or intermittent. It is actually double-edged: periodic, but *multiply* interrupted.

One would have expected /b/ and /p/ to behave in a way similar to the voiced and voiceless stops, respectively; but no such evidence exists in Fónagy's tables. Possibly, these two bilabial stops have additional (nonemotive) expressive potential that obscures the statistical effects of the expressive potential shared with the other stops. There seems to be such a possibility. In his discussion of the child's gradual acquisition of the arbitrary linguistic sign system, beginning with the first syllable /pa/, and ending with the whole phonological system of his mother tongue (see chapter 2), Jakobson (1968: 72) observes that "nasalization is especially charged with emotion in the child." "The oral stop, on the other hand, carries either less emotion or no emotion at all, and is not used for complaining, but for 'drawing attention, dismissing, refusing,' and as a calmer, more apathetic designation, and thereby signals the real transition from emotional expression to symbolic language" (73).

Since /pa/ is the first syllable acquired by the child for use as an arbitrary referential sign, and it contains the bilabial /p/, it is not implausible that precisely the bilabial stops are more conspicuously associated with these nonemotional moods, in addition to the other aspects of the expressive potential shared with the other oral stops. As suggested in chapter 2, the later the acquisition of a speech sound, the greater its potential for being used in onomatopoeia or emotive sound patterns.

It seems, then, highly plausible that the ENCODED~UNENCODED opposition is analogous in some way to the HARD~SOFT or RIGID~FLEXIBLE opposition, and that encoded corresponds to "hard" or "rigid." We should, however, again ask the question, why not match encoded with "soft," "flexible"? What perceptual qualities go with the ENCODED~UNENCODED opposition? Liberman et al. (1972) describe a series of experiments by Crowder and Morton (1969), who found that in auditory (but not visual) presentation, vowels produce a recency effect in certain cognitive tasks, but stops do not. Part of the explanation seems to be as follows:

> The special process that decodes the stops strips away all auditory information and presents to immediate perception a categorical linguistic event the listener can be aware of only as /b, d, g, p, t, or k/. Thus, there is for these segments no auditory, precategorical form that is available to consciousness for a time long enough to produce a recency effect. The relatively unencoded vowels, on the other hand, are capable of being perceived in a different way. . . . The listener can make relatively fine discriminations within phonetic classes because the auditory characteristics of the signal can

be preserved for a while. . . . In the experiment by Crowder, we may suppose that these same auditory characteristics of the vowel, held for several seconds in an echoic sensory register, provide the subject with rich, precategorical information that enables him to recall the most recently presented items with relative ease.

This passage draws attention to several aspects of the ENCODED~ UNENCODED opposition that can explain its perceptual corollaries. First, relatively unencoded sounds appear to have some kind of sensory rich-ness that highly encoded sounds lack. This intuitive observation can be explained by the assumption of Liberman and his colleagues that in the relatively unencoded sounds, the auditory characteristics of the signal, "the rich, precategorical information," can be preserved for a while in a "sensory register," whereas "the special process that decodes the stops strips away all auditory information and presents to immediate per-ception a categorical linguistic event." Several observations follow from this analysis. First, Hrushovski (1980: 39) mentions the insight formu-lated by I. A. Richards that poems are written with the "full body" of words; relatively unencoded sounds enable the language user to per-ceive a "fuller body" of words. Second, this sensory richness of the relatively unencoded sounds enables the listener to make fine discrimi-nations within phonetic classes. Third, all this increases the ease with which certain cognitive tasks are performed (not only the highly arti-ficial laboratory tasks that produced the recency effect in Crowder's experiment, but, possibly, also the task of reading; see Liberman and Mann, 1981: 128–29; Brady et al., 1983: 349–55; Mann, 1984: 1–10).

Now, the perception of rich sensory material and the making of fine distinctions precisely presuppose that openness, responsiveness, and susceptibility of adaptation characteristic of tender feelings and which seem to be lacking in aggressive behavior. Remaining firm in one's reliance on clear-cut categories and a lack of perceptiveness are impor-tant ingredients in a rigid and aggressive behavior. Reliance on rich precategorical information makes greater emotional and behavioral adaptability possible. It should be noted that Gestaltists (for example, Ehrenzweig, 1965) have observed that in visual designs clear-cut shapes assume a high degree of "plasticity" when perceived against a back-ground of shadings, "inarticulate scribbling," or, in the present termi-nology, rich precategorical information. This is particularly true when gestalt-free sensory material is subliminally perceived. The richer this precategorical sensory information, the greater the plasticity of the consciously perceived visual shapes. Once the inarticulate scribbling is rich enough to reach consciousness, the peculiar conscious quality of plasticity disappears. The same seems to be true, mutatis mutandis, of the sounds of the great masters of the violin. This underlying mechanism can explain the tender plasticity perceived in relatively lowly encoded consonants, which are, in fact, clear-cut linguistic categories perceived against a background of rich precategorical sensory information.

On Lateral Inhibition and Lingering Auditory Information

In light of the foregoing discussion and Crowder's more recent work, let us consider the following stanza from FitzGerald's *The Rubáiyát of Omar Khayyám*:

> Some for the Glories of This World; and some
> Sigh for the Prophet's Paradise to come;
> Ah, take the Cash, and let the Credit go,
> Nor heed the rumble of a distant Drum!

This quatrain is rich with euphonic sound patterns. Some of them are neutral as *the Prophet's Paradise* in line 2, or *Cash* and *Credit* in line 3 (where they are focused on words of symbolic significance). One is conspicuously onomatopoetic: *rumble . . . Drum*. It is the latter to which I wish to pay some attention. All the sounds of *rumble* (except for the /b/) are continuous and periodic—and relatively unencoded. The first three of them are repeated in *Drum*, in the same order. The /d/ of *Drum* too is heralded by *distant*, and less conspicuously by *heed* (in such a periodic context, the periodicity of the voicing in the stops /b, d/ also is foregrounded). One should notice one remarkable thing about the last line's sound pattern. The reader or listener is quite likely to become aware of the rich precategorical, periodic acoustic information and relate it to the rumble of the drum. In this way, the sound becomes "an echo of the sense," or, rather, the meaning and the acoustic structure reinforce the effect of similar features in each other. This observation seems the more remarkable owing to the fact that *Drum* is part of another sound pattern as well: it rhymes with *some* and *come*. Most readers who are aware of the rich precategorical auditory information in *Drum* report that they are not aware of a similar richness in the preceding rhyme-fellows.

Most of these observations on sound patterns do not go beyond the limits of more or less traditional literary criticism. However, Crowder's experiments may help explain the underlying cognitive mechanism. In a series of three experiments, the purpose of which was to find out whether the same kind of auditory memory supports both short-term memory and speech discrimination, Crowder (1982a) relied on the "suffix effect" (the results, by the way, strongly suggest that the same auditory memory underlies both faculties).

> The suffix effect is a decrement in recall of the last item in an immediate-memory list caused by an extra utterance (which does not have to be recalled). Since the paper by Crowder and Morton (1969) one influential hypothesis for this phenomenon has been that a verbal suffix damages information that otherwise remains available in sensory form, following auditory presentation. . . . The hypothesis is that speech sounds are represented, after they occur, on a two-dimensional, neurally spatial grid that is organized by input channel and time of arrival. . . . It is assumed that these representations are related to each other through the rules of re-current lateral inhibition. From this, it follows that after a series of utterances on the same physical channel (i.e., the same voice in the same location), there will be lingering auditory information about the most recent arrival. . . . The freedom of the last utterance in a series of retroactive lateral inhibition is held responsible for the large recency effect observed in immediate memory tests with auditory presentation, but not with visual presentation. (Crowder, 1982a: 477)

One interesting aspect of this phenomenon is that the decrement in recall occurs only when the suffix is verbal, say, the nonsense syllable *ba*, but not when it is nonverbal, say, a 1.000 Hz tone (the instructions to the subjects characterized the extra item, suffix, or tone as a cue telling people when to begin their recall attempt). There seems to be, then, an interference within the speech mode, but not between the speech mode and the nonspeech mode. A further remark of Crowder's concerns grouping: "When 'grouping,' for example, is used to explain something, the next question is always 'What causes grouping?' Indeed, an explanation of grouping in the auditory system might well rely on principles of lateral inhibition" (ibid., 477–78).

Coming back to FitzGerald's quatrain, we observe that the last three sounds of *Drum* are continuous and periodical, and less categorically perceptible than the stop sounds. So, when the word's meaning suggests some periodic but inarticulate auditory percept, the reader may employ one of the available cognitive strategies (as suggested by Repp, 1984, and others) to direct his attention from the phonetic category to the accessible precategorical auditory information and associate the two. The result is that some rich sonority is directly perceived in this word, consisting in auditory features and reinforced by semantic features. In light of Crowder's discussion, we may make two additional remarks. First, *Drum* is the last word of the quatrain, and so "there is lingering auditory information about the most recent arrival." Second, some grouping principle is also active here. The sonorant parts of the words *rumble* and *Drum* direct attention to the same kind of precategorical auditory information. So, instead of "contrastive interactions between auditory stimulus traces" (see Repp, 1984: 262), there may be some enhancing interaction between them. In other words, rather than inhibiting one another, the rich, precategorical auditory information appears to reinforce one another (these speculations have been supported by authorities in speech research).

These considerations appear to account, then, for the rich sensory or sonorant quality of the last line, especially the last word. The relative lack of perceived sonority in the preceding rhyme-fellows (*some* and *come*) appears to be due to the absence of the aspects considered here. But this difference between the rhyme-fellows—however obtrusive— appears to be in degree rather than in kind. One prominent reason for the auditory effect of *any* rhyme (even rhymes involving voiceless stops) seems to be a mutual reinforcement of similar auditory traces, some of which appear to linger on even after the recoding of the acoustic into the phonetic stream of information.

This issue may have far-reaching implications for understanding how rhyme and alliteration work in poetry. It is not yet sufficiently understood, and much empirical research must be done before we can make some confident assertions in these respects. I have consulted two leading experts on issues related to lateral inhibition. As I understand their answers, they seem to support my speculations to *some* extent. I take the liberty to reproduce relevant parts of those answers. Bruno Repp of the Haskins Laboratories writes:

> The theory predicts that inhibition will be maximal when there is moderate similarity, and minimal when there is either great similarity or great dissimilarity. This follows from the principle that a stimulus generates a positive neural response surrounded by an

inhibitory area of negative polarity. If a subsequent stimulus falls
in the center (i.e., is very similar to the preceding stimulus), it may
generate an enhanced response, because of integration with the
previous response; if it falls in the inhibitory region (i.e., is moderately similar) it will be reduced; if it falls outside that area, it
will be unaffected. Thus lateral inhibition theory has no difficulty
accounting for the detection of similarities. (personal communication)

I propose to adduce a possible example. Chapter 2 is called "On Musicality in Verse and Phonological Universals." Both phrases contain the
stem *vers*. This is rarely realized since it occurs in a prose discourse. I
myself realized the sound pattern only a few minutes after I coined the
title, and even now I sometimes think of it without realizing the sound
pattern. This depends on my way of performing the phrase. In a similar
fashion, people are rarely aware that the words *tail* and *tailor* contain
the same sequence of three phonemes. Both the sequence *tail* and *vers*
are pronounced as shorter in the longer word, and there may be other
articulational differences as a corollary, such as coarticulation of /i/
and /v/. This may be, I assume, an instance of "moderately similar"
stimuli. Now, if the word *Universals* is pronounced with a slight "hesita-
tion pause" after *Uni-*, and the syllable is prolonged to match the length
of the monosyllabic, the stimulus is rendered *very similar* to the preceding stimulus and "an enhanced response, because of integration with
the previous response" is actively experienced, especially when one
"climbs" back to the same intonational pitch in pronouncing the second
verse. Similarity of pitch, however, does not seem to be indispensable
for the effect. Robert G. Crowder of Yale University comments on the
acoustic-phonetic mechanism underlying such phenomena:

> The lateral inhibition model specifically includes the possibility
> that if the two sounds residing together in auditory memory are
> close enough to one another, acoustically, their effect will combine
> rather than engage in inhibition. There would be precedent for
> the assumption that the total effect would be the larger for having
> had a repeated sound. This depends on my assumption that the
> inhibitory interaction takes place within the formant energy of
> the words, even though they may be spoken at different pitches.
> (personal communication)

I find this a very stimulating assumption. It may account for the lingering rich precategorical acoustic information sometimes so strongly experienced in the reading of poetry (as, for instance, the "enhanced response" to *the rumble of a distant Drum*). However, as suggested by both Repp and Crowder, the issues raised here require further extensive experimenting. One such issue concerns the question, how to determine the borderlines between "very similar," "moderately similar," and "dissimilar." This seems to be an empirical question. In the essay "On Musicality in Verse," Kenneth Burke (1957c) considers a set of devices for what he calls "concealed alliteration" in poetic passages from Coleridge "that seem to have a marked consistency of texture" (296). These devices include "the repetition of a sound in cognate variation, acrostic scrambling, chiasmus, augmentation and diminution" (299). His introductory example of "the repetition of a sound in cognate variation" is "bathed by the mist" where, he says, if we take into account the "close phonetic relationship between *b* and *m* as phonetic cognates, we find that 'b- b- the m-' is a *concealed* alliteration. 'B- b- the b-' would be blunt and even relatively tiresome. . . . And were 'mist' replaced by some word beginning with a phonetically disrelated sound, such as *w*, *z*, or *k*, the particular kind of musical bracketing that the poet got here would be lost" (296). He proposes for such concealed alliterations the term *colliteration*. We may next note an acrostic structure for getting consistency with variation.

> In "tyrannous and strong," for instance, the consonant structure of the third word is but the rearrangement of the consonant structure in the first: *t-r-n-s* is reordered as *s-t-r-ng*. In the line, . . . "beneath the burthen" has a similar scrambling: *b-n-th* (unvoiced), *b-th* (voiced)-*n*. Perhaps the most beautiful example of consonantal acrostic in Coleridge is the line from "Kubla Khan": "A damsel with a dulcimer," where you match *d-m-z-l* with *d-l-s-m* plus *r*. (298)

As an example of *chiasmus*, Burke quotes "Dupes of a deep delusion," which is "*oo* of an *ee ee oo*." From music Burke borrows the terms augmentation and diminution.

> In poetry, then, you could get the effect of augmentation by first giving two consonants in juxtaposition and then repeating them in the same order but separated by the length of a vowel. Thus in

> She sent the gentle sleep from Heaven,

> That slid into my soul,

you find the *sl* progression in "sleep," "slid," and "soul," but it is varied in its third appearance by augmentation: *sl*, *sl*, *s-l*. As an instance of the contrary process, diminution, we have

> But silently, by slow degrees,

where the temporal space between the *s* and *l* in "silently" is collapsed in "slow": *s-l*, *sl*. (299)

Some of these devices present more similar stimuli, some of them less. One could construct along Burke's categories a scale of decreasing similarity. The crucial issue would be to determine the borderlines between very similar, moderately similar, and dissimilar. The answer to this question will determine whether in a certain instance of repeated sound patterns it is inhibitory, or enhancing, interaction that takes place within the formant energy of the words. The issue can be settled only by extensive empirical testing.

Another problem raised by Repp that requires further extensive testing is even more crucial. Do we experience the rich precategorical sensory information only in vocal performances or in silent performances as well? If there is no difference, the phenomena we are interested in are not really auditory in nature. The answer seems to be that we also experience it in silent performances *of a certain kind*.

Two things are very clear to me in this matter. First, when people perform poetry, they read it in a different way in many important respects from "normal" speech (see my discussion of *verse* and *universals* above). I have discussed some of these differences at considerable length elsewhere (Tsur, 1977). On the whole, for the special poetic effects to be perceptible, usually a much clearer articulation is needed than the one usual in, say, casual conversation. Second, the performance of poetry involves in one way or another the activation of some mechanisms that are closely associated with auditory perception. I am using such roundabout phrasing because I am not sure that actual vocalization is needed for what we are up to. Suppose you ask someone, "Can you tell which sound is higher, /s/ or /š/—without vocalizing them?" I, personally, can clearly "hear" the difference, even when carefully avoiding any sort of vocalization. It is, however, quite puzzling that my "percepts" are considerably clearer if I allow my tongue to be in the correct position for the articulation of these two speech sounds. This may have to do with the phenomena accounted for by the motor theory of speech perception. In any event, these perceptions are not available in just *any* performance, but only in a performance in which *some* such introspective strategy is followed. I am quite confident that experienced readers of poetry, including even professors of literature, cannot have significant intuitions about the sound structure of poetry because they read it as they do any other verbal discourse.

In the Haskins Laboratories' *Status Report on Speech Research SR-/83*, Michael Studdert-Kennedy (1985) adduces some evidence that might prove crucial in dealing with this problem. He summarizes reports by Cambell and Dodd and by Spoehr and Corin, who "found significant recency and suffix effects for the lip-read but not for the graphic lists." It was also found that "a lip-read suffix reduced recall of auditorily presented lists. Evidently, speech heard, but not seen, and speech seen, but not heard, share a common representation" (57). If Studdert-Kennedy is right in explaining this phenomenon via the decoder's own articulatory apparatus, I may be right in my speculation. However, further extensive empirical testing is needed to establish, first of all, the actual responses of real readers of poetry.

Consonant Symbolism and Vowel Symbolism

The attentive reader may have noticed what appears to be an inconsistency between my description of aggressive consonants and aggressive vowels. The aggressive quality of voiceless stops can be explained by the absence of undifferentiated rich precategorical sensory information, whereas the aggressive quality of back vowels is precisely explained by the relatively undifferentiated perception of their first and second formants, which are closer to one another than those of the front vowels. There is, however, no inconsistency here at all. It is only an additional indication that we must "fix our attention not on likeness of elements, but on structural relationships within a scale or a matrix," as suggested by Gombrich. There is nothing inherently tender or aggressive in undifferentiated percepts. One may, however, expect that undifferentiated percepts tend to be perceived as more emotional than differentiated ones.

So, *if* we have the scale or opposition DIFFERENTIATED~UNDIFFERENTIATED, and the scale or opposition EMOTIONAL~NONEMOTIONAL, and *if* we appear to have reasons to perceive the two scales as somehow analogous, we should expect that the nonemotional end of one scale is matched with the differentiated end of the other (we still lack, however, a reasonably elaborate and consistent theory to account for our having or not having reasons to perceive two scales or oppositions as somehow analogous).

On the other hand, *if* we have reasons to perceive the DIFFERENTI-ATED~UNDIFFERENTIATED scale as somehow analogous to the DARK~BRIGHT scale, we should expect to associate the undifferentiated end of one scale with the dark end of the other. *If*, now, we have reasons to perceive some further analogy between these two scales and a scale of emotions, we may expect to find that the differentiated end of the first scale is associated with the end of bright emotions, whereas the undifferentiated end is associated with the end of dark emotions. Viewed from this angle of structural relationships, one should see no contradiction between the association of differentiated percepts with both bright emotions and nonemotional states of mind. The stream of acoustic information is far less differentiated than the phonetic category it carries, even in the case of front vowels. So, the mere attending back from the clear-cut phonetic category to the rich precategorical sensory information may be interpreted as a shift to the emotional aspects of the information, while further discrimination between more and less differentiated sensory information may be interpreted as the discrimination between brighter and darker emotions. On the other hand, when attending to the precategorical sensory information is a given, the opposition UNDIFFERENTIATED~DIFFERENTIATED is interpreted as analogous to the EMOTIONAL~NONEMOTIONAL opposition. Language-users seem capable of freely switching back and forth between these two attitudes on promptings of the contents of the message. When dark emotions are associated with the high energy pole of the scale of energy levels, the perceptual outcome may be interpreted, in proper circumstances, as aggressive.

Vowels are uninterrupted streams of energy; the same is true, typically, of emotional mental processes (hence, the intuitive acceptability of the foregoing structural relationships). Consonants, on the other hand, whether continuous or abrupt, are streams of energy obstructed to some degree. While there are no significant differences between the various vowels in respect to accessibility of the stream of acoustic information to perception, there are substantial differences between the various consonants. Likewise, whereas all vowels are not only continuous but periodic, some continuous consonants are periodic and some are aperiodic. Consequently, some types of structural relationships that

are felt to exist between certain vowel oppositions and certain oppositions of emotional or perceptual qualities are less readily available (or
completely unavailable) for analogies between consonant oppositions
and oppositions of emotional or perceptual qualities.

To account for the analogy between certain moods and certain
speech sounds, one must postulate an additional level of cognitive organization: the *strategy of categorization*. There is *rapid* and *delayed* categorization. The former consists in achieving a stable category based on
a minimum of precategorical information; the latter lingers on rich
precategorical information before categorization.

Certain moods, such as aggression and cheerfulness, seem to be disposed to cope with reality by the strategy of rapid categorization. Likewise, voiceless stops appear to reflect aggression as well as cheerfulness.
When the reader of a poem perceives in it a more frequent than average distribution of highly encoded consonants, while the contents of
the poem reflect some mood disposed toward rapid categorization such
as aggression or cheerfulness, he may relate the similar psychological
atmospheres resulting from rapid categorization as associated with the
mood and sound pattern. What appears to be the factor common to the
moods disposed toward rapid categorization is the high energy level
involved. This may explain how anger is related to cheerfulness and
tender feelings to sorrow.

Turning to back vowels, acoustically they are undifferentiated as
compared to front vowels. Undifferentiatedness is typically associated
with emotional states of mind. In the context of back vowels, we might
speak of some dark emotion—sorrow, anger, mystery. When back vowels abound in a poem, coupled with high energy (derived from prosodic, syntactic, or semantic resources), the reader may perceive—in
the appropriate thematic context—some aggressive quality. When back
vowels abound in a poem with low energy level, the reader may tend
to perceive in it some sad quality, some mysterious atmosphere, or the
like—depending on the thematic and semantic context.

[±Periodic] Double-Edgedness of Sibilants

We still need to explain the consistent emotional difference between
periodic and aperiodic consonants. It seems to be well established that
[±PERIODIC] is analogous with [±TENDER], coupling the positive with
the positive and the negative with the negative values of the two di-

chotomies. How should we account for this analogy? To say that aperiodic sounds are noises, or that periodic sounds are musical whereas aperiodic sounds are harsh, seems to be true, but explains nothing: it merely restates the issue.

Periodic sounds have been described (May and Repp, 1982: 145) as "the recurrence of signal portions with similar structure," whereas aperiodic stimuli have been said to have "randomly changing waveform" that "may have more idiosyncratic features to be remembered." The recurring signal portions with similar structures may arouse in the perceiver a relatively relaxed kind of attentiveness (there will be no surprises; one may expect the same waveform to recur). Thus, periodic sounds are experienced as smoothly flowing. The randomly changing waveforms of aperiodic sounds, with their "idiosyncratic features," are experienced as disorder, as a disruption of the "relaxed kind of attentiveness." Thus, aperiodic sounds are experienced as harsh, strident, turbulent, and the like. Some of these adjectives are, indeed, frequently used in the phonetic description of the aperiodic continuants. Thus, Halle (1978: 296) speaks of a mechanism "that produces strident sounds, such as /f v s z š ž č ǰ/, and distinguishes them from the rest. It consists in directing the air stream against the sharp edges of the upper teeth, thereby producing audible turbulence." Jakobson and Waugh (1979: 139) describe this mechanism as follows: "The optimal noisiness, achieved by a supplementary obstacle in the way of the airstream and a consequent intensified turbulence, opposes the strident obstruents to the nonstrident (mellow) ones."

We have reached a point of accounting for the notorious doubleedgedness of the sibilants. On the one hand, sound patterns based on /s, š/ may serve as sound imitations of natural noises of varying volumes (ranging from the rustling of curtains to the roar of the sea); on the other hand, they may have a tender, hushing quality. This doubleedgedness seems to be derived from the phenomenon observed—these consonants offer alternative cognitive strategies to direct our attention to the linguistic category or to the auditory information that carries it. The tender or hushing quality of /s, š/ may have to do with their feature [+CONTINUOUS] and with their being among the few consonants that need little restructuring in the phonetic decoding of the signal, enabling the perceiver to attend to some rich, inarticulate sensory information. Their noisy quality springs from the aperiodic nature of this sensory information. The feature [-VOICED] will be interpreted in the strident context as *lack* of sonority, richness, or smoothness; in the hushing context it may be interpreted as having an onomatopoetic element, the imitation of whispering.

To test the explanatory power of this discussion, I propose to consider one issue in Snyder's remarkable little book (1930), devoted to a group of poems described by the author as "hypnotic," or "spell-weaving," or "trance-inducing." Snyder argues that "certain poems have a peculiar trance-inducing technique; that they owe their mysterious 'spell' to a magic no more incomprehensible than that of hypnotism; that by intensifying the listeners' suggestibility they permit experiences where—for better or for worse—the poet holds sway over the listeners' conscious and subconscious mind" (Snyder, 1930: 38).

I shall not go into the details of Snyder's theory and critical practice, nor shall I indicate where I agree or disagree with his assumptions. I only wish to pay some attention to one of his favorite examples, his discussion of Gray's "Elegy Written in a Country Churchyard." Let us follow his description of the first quatrain, which he considers to be "one of the most harmonious stanzas." "The metre is iambic with only two such slight departures from regularity as serve to keep it from being painfully mechanical" (51).

> The vowel effects are singularly interesting; but as the present state of knowledge on the psychological effectiveness of "dark" and "light" vowels is rather dubious, I will not risk giving evidence on this point, however tantalizing the temptation may be. But the consonantal effects—to consider only the most obvious ones— are, I think, unique. Even Poe with his adroit choice of the name "Lenore" and his rather artificial coinage of the name "Ulalume," never quite equaled the skill with which liquids and nasals are repeated in the *Elegy*. . . . Thus, a careful inspection shows that in these four lines every accented syllable save one—and it is the accented syllables that really count—either ends in a vowel sound or involves a liquid or a nasal! . . . Liquids and nasals are capitalized.

> the cuRfew toLLs the kNeLL of paRtiNG day,
> the LowiNG heRd wiNd sLowLy o'eR the Lea,
> the pLowMaN hoMewaRd pLods his weaRy way.
> aNd Leaves the woRLd to daRkNess aNd to Me.

The second and third stanzas, like the first, continue, so far as versification is concerned, to employ the very highest artistry to satisfy and soothe the ear; and, with only slight modification, the same thing may be said of the whole poem. (Snyder, 1930: 51–52)

Let us consider Snyder's observation that "every accented syllable save one . . . either ends in a vowel sound or involves a liquid or a nasal." What vowels, nasals, and liquids have in common is that all are acoustically periodical. One could add here that the semi-vowels prominent in the words loWing, ploWman, and waY are periodical too. Snyder only vaguely indicates what the significance of this observation may be (that even Poe never quite equaled this skill, and that it had to do with "soothing the ear"). Now, the significance of Snyder's observation on vowels, liquids, and nasals in Gray's "Elegy" will become apparent when we realize that Snyder pointed out some of the characteristics of hypnotic poetry in terms that are very similar to our description of periodic and aperiodic sounds. Two such aspects of hypnotic poetry are mentioned in "as the early portions of such hypnotic poems skilfully *avoid* whatever is '*startling*,' they preserve a marked *regularity of rhythm*" (41); and again, "Another point in which practically all of these poems show an interesting parallel to hypnotism is their freedom from any abrupt changes which would be likely to break the spell, and especially freedom from such ideas as compel mental alertness." It will be remembered that periodic sounds have been characterized as "the recurrence of signal portions with similar structure," which on a miniature scale is akin to "regularity of rhythm" on a larger scale. Likewise, aperiodic sounds have been characterized as having a "randomly changing waveform" that "may have more idiosyncratic features to be remembered." This seems to be akin, on the minute acoustic level, to what has been characterized on the level of ideas as abrupt changes that compel mental alertness skillfully avoided by hypnotic poetry. It will be remembered that we have compared the effects of periodic to aperiodic sounds as follows: "The recurring signal portions with similar structures may arouse in the perceiver a relatively relaxed kind of attentiveness (there will be no surprises; one may expect the same waveform to recur). Thus, periodic sounds are experienced as smoothly flowing. The randomly changing waveforms of aperiodic sounds, with their 'idiosyncratic features,' are experienced as disorder, as a disruption of the relaxed kind of attentiveness." Thus, it seems quite plausible that Snyder may have intuitively felt that vowels, liquids, and nasals in prominent positions in a hypnotic poem reinforce on the subphonemic acoustic level a quality that is typically felt in such poems on other, more easily discernible levels. The prominence of such periodic sounds in stressed syllables is *not* an indispensable characteristic of what Snyder calls "hypnotic" poetry; but once it is there, it may greatly enhance the effects noted on the more palpable levels. It seems to render the effect somehow more evasive.[6]

Dental~Palatal Articulatory Gestures

I have discussed at great length two aspects of the relationship between the acoustic and phonetic stream of information in speech sounds. On one hand, we *attend away*, typically, *from* the acoustic information to the abstract phonetic category which is thus typically stripped of all sensuous attributes. On the other hand, the various perceptual and emotional qualities regularly perceived in speech sounds by a very wide range of speakers can be explained by the assumption that *some* of the rich precategorical sensory information *does* reach awareness, subliminally though: we seem to attend back to the acoustic stream of information. This is a cognitive way to account for the "mysterious" emotional and perceptual qualities of speech sounds. There is another way implied in the foregoing discussion which, on closer inspection, turns out to be a specific instance of the same general principle. We *attend away from* the articulatory gesture *to* the abstract phonetic category produced by it. But some of the perceptual and emotional qualities regularly perceived in speech sounds by a wide range of speakers can be explained by the assumption that we *attend back from* the abstract phonetic category *to* the articulatory gesture that produced it. That the present book is devoted mainly to the first mode of explanation does not imply that I consider it less important; rather, it reflects my preoccupation during the past few years, and that little or no work has been done until now along these lines. This section, however, will be devoted to the examination of one issue, implicit in the opposition DENTAL~PALATAL, in its own right, as well as a paradigmatic exploration of how articulatory gestures can be utilized in the kind of explanation we are engaged in throughout this book (a second issue, some expressive resources implicit in the articulation of /r/, will be discussed in chapter 5).

Palatal consonants are among the latest acquired by young children;

---

6. For a somewhat more elaborate discussion of hypnotic poetry, see Tsur, 1992, chapter 18.

so, as suggested in chapter 2, one may expect them to have an unusually great potential for being used in sound-gestures or onomatopoeia. Some of these sound-gestures are formalized or lexicalized in adult speech, but some—though informal and spontaneous—give rise to rather consistent and widespread intuitions. Thus, for instance, Fónagy (1983: 59–62, 72) has found that subjects of varying age groups, in several languages, whether with normal hearing or born deaf, find that the palatal stop /t̆/ (as in "Tuesday") is *wetter* than its dental counterpart /t/; the same holds true of /n̆/ (as in "new"), as opposed to /n/, or /d̆/ (as in "duty") as opposed to /d/. Fónagy (personal communication) suggests that the only way to account for this common intuition is with reference to the increased area of contact of two necessarily wet surfaces in articulating the palatal consonants.

The increased area of contact of two surfaces, characteristic of palatal consonants, also carries some emotional information. It suggests that the particular emotional character of palatal consonants is derived from the opposition of this articulatory gesture to its counterpart in the dental stops /n, t, d/. The opposition is between a *broad area* of contact (in palatals) and a well-defined, *clear-cut point* of contact in the dental stop. Now, the creation of such a clear-cut, well-determined point of contact (as opposed to a broad area of contact) can be interpreted (or rather perceived) as a gesture characterized by a sense of control and precision, firmness and determination, being set in purpose; whereas the creation of a broad area of contact tends to be perceived as a gesture of opposite character. It would appear that precisely this character of the articulatory gesture underlying palatal consonants has been lexicalized in the Hungarian adjective "*tutyi-mutyi*," which means "softy"; it suggests feebleness or even debility—or at least irresolution—in the actions of the referent, and indicates an attitude of derision in the speaker. This attitude is enhanced by the dissimilation of the initial consonants that renders the iterative reinforcements more sharply discernible and at times imparts to the reduplication an ironical, disparaging, inflated character (cf. Jakobson and Waugh, 1979: 196–97). We should be, indeed, surprised if the word meant, for example, "strenuous."

Palatal sound gestures, however, even when publicly shared, are not always lexicalized or even formalized. A central issue in Mark Liberman's discussion (1979) of the intonation system of English is what he calls "the children's chant" of American children. "Its most familiar instantiation is perhaps on the taunting nonsense string 'nyah, nyah, nyah, nyah, nyah'" (ibid., 32). Here, too, the broad area of contact imparts to the articulatory gesture underlying the initial palatal consonants—and eventually to the whole nonsense string—a similar ironical, disparaging character.

To what extent can we hold this disparaging character responsible for a rather persistent association of palatalization with diminutive forms? In Nootka, for instance, some physical characteristics of the person addressed or spoken of are implied in speech partly by consonantal play. A "diminutive suffix is used in addition to some consonantal modification of the words to characterize beings with visible blemishes. People who are abnormally small (for example, dwarfs) are spoken of with (in addition to the suffix) a palatalization (sharpening) of all hissing and hushing sibilants" (Jakobson and Waugh, 1979: 205). Such a usage may appear rather odd to a person brought up in Western culture. Nevertheless,

> An approximative analogue to this kind of word-building with a suffix and with a sound change could perhaps be seen in the German treatment of the diminutive suffix -*chen* which . . . also involves an unusual consonantal alteration. But German, in contradistinction to Nootka, manifests the alteration in the suffix itself. At the beginning of this diminutive suffix there appears a palatal continuant different from the corresponding velar continuant occurring in the same sound sequence elsewhere: thus, only this sound difference discriminates two words: *Kuhchen* "little cow" has a palatal continuant at the beginning of the diminutive suffix -*chen* added to the root *Kuh* "cow," while *Kuchen* "cake" has a velar continuant.

One thing, however, should be noted. Far from taunting, the German diminutive –*chen* expresses affection; still, this affection is mingled into a general attitude of superiority—or rather a general attitude of attributing relative weakness to the object of affection.

We might mention two further instances. An acquaintance of mine had the idiosyncrasy—presumably under the influence of German—of palatalizing velar continuants and hushing sibilants when talking, in Hebrew and Hungarian, to small children. Another rare example "of European use of a productive sound symbolic ablaut is the Basque formation of diminutives by the sharpening (palatalizing) of dentals and sometimes velars" (ibid., 201).

So, as I have insisted throughout this book, speech perception is based on the fact that we attend away from the acoustic information that reaches our ear to the articulatory gesture that produced it; and from the articulatory gesture to the intended abstract phonetic category. The articulatory gesture is more easily accessible to introspection and consciousness than the acoustic information (hence the greater "mysteriousness" of those perceptual and emotional qualities of sounds that are based on the subliminal perception of acoustic information). When people have an evasive feeling that palatal consonants are somehow "wetter" than their dental counterparts, it can readily be accounted for in terms of articulatory gestures. Relative wetness seems to be only a secondary attribute of a more fundamental opposition: that of the relative size of the area of contact between articulatory surfaces. The smaller the area of contact, the stronger the feeling of precision, determinateness, and the sense of control (when we hear a person sharpening the area of contact between the tip of the tongue and the alveolar ridge in articulating the dental stops, we tend to infer behind it a dominant, authoritative, determined personality). And, conversely, the broader the contact area between the tongue and the palate, the greater the feeling of imprecision, of a lack of sense of control, of inaccuracy, or of general inadequacy.

We may conclude, first, that when the articulatory gestures underlying the opposition DENTAL~PALATAL reaches consciousness from behind the perception of phonetic categories, it is perceived as part of some more general body language. Second, since the palatal consonants are acquired relatively late by young children, they are much more prone to be used in onomatopoeia and sound gestures; thus, the emotional quality is much more readily detected in the palatal consonants than the opposite kind of quality in dental consonants (this is another way of saying that palatal consonants are more *marked* than the dental ones).

It should be noticed that the opposition between articulatory gestures is perceived as analogous to an opposition between moods or attitudes that are *highly generalized*, such as "strenuous" versus "feeble" or, even more vaguely, "superior" versus "inferior." Thus, the nonsense string "nyah-nyah-nyah-nyah-nyah" in the children's chant achieves its taunting tone by attributing to the addressee some very vague kind of feebleness, inadequacy, or inferiority and expressing, by the same token, a vague feeling of superiority of the "chanters." It is only when the sound gestures involved in palatalization are lexicalized, as in Hungarian "*tutyi-mutyi*," or formalized as in Nootka when speaking to or of dwarfs, that they assume some more specific content, whether on the abstraction level of STRENUOUS~FEEBLE or SUPERIOR~INFERIOR.

Some Wider Implications

To conclude, I wish to point out a few wider implications of this discussion for poetic theory. Taxonomy and statistical investigations give us a general orientation. But to explain more specific intuitions about poetic phenomena in their uniqueness, we need a *creative* or perhaps *generative* model capable of handling a potentially infinite set of (poetic) utterances. Such a creative model is needed to account for the observed relation between the two streams of information, *phonetic* and *semantic*, in expressive sound patterns. Our ability to handle novel cases seems to be derived from two sources: a general knowledge of how to combine units from the two streams of information, and a highly creative capability of abstracting the combinational potential of those units from their relevant features. With many of these features and their combinational potential, we may be familiar from past literary experience; but in novel circumstances we seem to abstract at least some of them in unforeseen ways from unforeseen resources. Furthermore, past experience as an explanation for our capability of handling certain familiar combinations is a red herring: it diverts attention from the fact that we still have to explain how we handled the particular combination of those semantic and phonetic features when it was novel to us.

These processes draw upon a pool of acquired linguistic knowledge, but also upon a pool of "knowledge unlearned and untaught," to use Halle's phrase (1978), some of which seems to be a grammar "written in the language of physiology" (Liberman, 1970: 315). To describe this, one needs to go outside the boundaries of traditional poetics to the areas investigated by linguistics and cognitive science.

Cognitive poetics is, then, more than just another alternative language in which the facts of poetics may be described. Traditional poetics have important things to say about how the sound units and meaning units are combined. But we need the various branches of cognitive science to account for the combinational potential of these units, and it is this potential that both shapes and constrains the intuitive process of combination. As my analysis of the mechanism underlying the statistical correlations between back vowels and such qualities as "mystic obscurities" and "hatred and struggle" may suggest, far from being confined to nonaesthetic processes, cognitive poetics provides powerful tools for understanding the relationship between aesthetic qualities and their nonaesthetic perceptual conditions as well as the significant relationships between two or more aesthetic qualities.

≋≋ **2** On Musicality in

Verse and Phonological Universals

Musicality seems to be the most salient—if not the distinctive—property of poetry. The principles of musicality in verse have solidified in handbooks of versification into easily manageable rules. Unfortunately, however, such rules can hardly tell us the difference between, say, Milton's "miraculous organ voice" and the flatness of the verse by some of his imitators (see Tsur, 1977: 215–38). The problem is infinitely multiplied if we come to close readings of, say, French Symbolist poetry, where "mere" semantic analysis and semantic discussions appear sometimes ridiculously beside the point. When in such a plight, we often find that critics, students, or university professors would make either some general comment on the poet's great mastery or on the impossibility to deal with the musicality of the poem, or they would make a more specific statement on the quality of some sound that would hardly hold water in a consistency test. A random browsing through Henri Peyre's discussions of French Symbolist poems in Burnshaw's popular collection (1964) came up with the following crop. Baudelaire's "Harmonie du Soir" is "a masterpiece of musicality in poetry. . . . The music of words and rimes ingeniously interwoven cannot, of course, be adequately conveyed by a literal translation" (ibid., 14). "The three initial *v* sounds in line 1 are like piercing arrows of pain" (ibid., 15); in line 4, nonetheless, "the *v* and *l* sounds are subtly blended" (ibid.). In Verlaine's "Clair de Lune," "the first stanza is filled with broad, calm, doleful *a* sounds" (ibid., 37), whereas in the sonnet "Le Vierge et le Vivace et le Belle Aujourd'hui," "Mallarmé's art stands at its highest. . . .

All the rimes are in *i* or *ui*, a sound which has something of the angular sharpness of ice itself" (ibid., 55). Sometimes we hear comments on the "beautiful" sounds of a poem (more rarely on its "ugly" sounds). However, before the scientific impartiality of linguistic description all speech sounds are equal. Nonetheless, for readers of poetry it is difficult to escape the feeling that some speech sounds are more equal. In what follows, I shall take up the notion that some speech sounds are more musical, more emotional, or more beautiful than others and attempt to anchor those judgments in a system of phonological universals in such a way that they can be maintained more or less consistently.

Phonological Universals

Roman Jakobson's remarkable little book (1968), *Child Language, Aphasia, and Phonological Universals*, first published in German in 1941, laid the foundations of later structuralist phonology, establishing a model that appears to have considerable psychological reality. As I shall claim, this phonological model can account for a variety of literary phenomena. It presents the reader with certain universal laws of phonological dynamics as abstracted from the sequence of children's mastering speech, the reversed sequence of aphatics' forgetting speech, and the same laws of "solidarity" as related in the languages of the world (later termed "markedness"). As there are no cases found in which the use of, say, the vowel /y/ (ü) has been acquired before /u/, or /u/ forgotten before /y/—no language has been found in which the vowel /y/ exists but not /u/, or the vowel /ø/ (ö) but not /o/.

The dynamics underlying Jakobson's model involve a series of splits of the undifferentiated mass of sounds into contrasts realized by the speaker. A remarkable thing about the way children learn to speak is that in a prelanguage phase of babbling, each child provides ample evidence that he may have at his disposal all the sounds existing in all the languages of the world. Afterward, suddenly, he forgets, as it seems, his whole repertoire, and as the first step to speech he learns to distinguish between consonants and vowels. This contrast appears in its sharpest possible manifestation in saying /pa/. /p/ is a voiceless consonant, pronounced by a maximum closure of the lips, /a/ is a vowel (voiced by its very nature), pronounced by a maximum opening of the lips. The next two oppositions of consonants the child acquires are ORAL~NASAL and LABIAL~DENTAL, usually in this order (hence, the basic vocabulary of children in many languages, *papa*, *mama*, *tata*, *nana*; "by the repetition

of the same syllable, children signal that their phonation is not babbling, but a verbal message," [Jakobson and Waugh, 1979: 196]). The
vowels split in two directions, along the /a/~/u/ line (WIDE~NARROW),
and the /u/~/i/ line (ROUNDED~UNROUNDED). The first split has been
felt to involve a perceptual contrast between CHROMATIC~ACHROMATIC,
the latter between dark and light vowels.

Of unusually great interest are some of Jakobson's observations on
the differentiation between the denotative and expressive use of speech
sounds. While the child proceeds with mastering the "arbitrary linguistic signs," selecting and contrasting sounds—being "inseparably linked
to the sign nature of language"—he constantly resorts to the other
sounds, still unmastered, for sound gestures (interjections and onomatopoeia). Children use certain sounds for onomatopoetic function
"while they continue to replace them in their remaining vocabulary."
When this distinction is not realized by linguists, they find great confusion in the process of children's acquiring speech. "Sound gestures,
which tend to form a layer apart even in the language of the adult,
appear to seek out those sounds which are inadmissible in a given language" (Jakobson, 1968: 25–26). Nasal vowels are among the child's
latest acquisitions and are rare in the world's languages. Indeed, "nasalization is especially charged with emotion in the child" (ibid., 72). "The
oral stop, on the other hand, carries either less emotion or no emotion at all, and is not used for complaining, but for 'drawing attention,
dismissing, refusing,' and as a calmer, more apathetic designation, and
thereby signals the real transition from emotional expression to symbolic language" (ibid., 75).

Jakobson's book was first published over forty years ago. To what extent can it still be regarded as valid today? Studdert-Kennedy (1982)
suggests the answer in a review-article of a conference of thirty-four
linguists and psychologists during May 1978 ("a compendium of theory
and research done over the previous decade in the young field of child
phonology"). Jakobson's theories are cited (and disputed) in ten of the
thirteen chapters in volume 1 (ibid., 511). As for its historical merits,
Studdert-Kennedy quotes one of the papers: "Child phonology begins
with the publication of Jakobson's *Kindersprache, Aphasie, und Allgemeine
Lautgesetze* in 1941" (ibid., 510). Another paper suggests that "the entire
cautious and meticulous modern tradition of child phonology field-
work was forged by the necessity" of establishing counterevidence to
Jakobson's arguments (ibid., 511). In view of this, Jakobson's model
weathered remarkably well. Two of the papers produced data that dis-

count Jakobson's claim of discontinuity between babbling and speech, a discontinuity that is more apparent than real (ibid., 510); and several produced evidence that "there does seem to be much more cross-language and within-language variations than Jakobson would predict" (ibid., 511). But on the level required for my ensuing argument, Jakobson's model seems to have been upheld to a remarkable extent.

Phonological Regression

One of the virtues of a good developmental model is that it can give insight into the nature of regressions. Those to be discussed here also can be accounted for within the general framework of psychoanalytic theory; but Jakobson's cognitive model can describe and predict their specific details. This, of course, is an enormous advantage for the practical critic. To understand the aesthetic relevance of these regressions, it is enough to note that poetry has to do with both pleasure and the expression of emotions.

According to psychoanalytic theory, one possible source of pleasure is regression to a level of functioning characteristic of an earlier age. Kris and Gombrich (1965) contend that the scribbling style of caricature involves regression to the infantile pleasure of exploring articulate motor activities, just as punning and nonsense talk involve regression to prelanguage babbling. It is plausible that the phonetic aspects of poetry afford such pleasure in the exploration of meaningless sounds in a publicly respectable medium. Similarly, Ehrenzweig (1965) asserts that in painting and music there are articulate gestalts appealing to our "surface mind," and inarticulate, thing-free scribblings and sounds appealing to our "depth mind." We may add with Jakobson that in child language there are two distinct uses of sound: *referential*, which is nonemotional, and *expressive*, making use of sounds that are not yet used for "arbitrary linguistic signs." In poetic language we have both mounted one on top of the other. Sounds are combined into words by a "syntagmatic" relationship (Jakobson, 1968: 70), "forming entities of linguistic value" (ibid., 25). At the same time there is a nonreferential combination of sounds, based on repetition, forming reference-free—*thing-free*, so to speak—qualities, exploiting not so much differentiated *contrasting features* as similarities. Literary critics sometimes merely point out that these repetitions are there. In several earlier studies I have pointed out how these poetic repetitions may *converge* or *diverge* to constitute some compact sound pattern or generate a diffuse, thing-free sound texture and contribute to the witty or emotional quality of a poem (see Tsur, 1978; 1977: 175–214; 1983b: 11–15; 1992, chapter 4). In this chapter I am proposing distinctions for describing sound effects in poetry that are derived from Jakobson's model.

The following problem arises in connection with regression to infantile pleasure in sounds: can we distinguish "mere" regression to infantile pleasure from a structured regression? Before answering, let us consider some instances of "mere" regression.

"Thus we find . . . a considerable number of babbling words in the vocabulary of all languages taken over from the nursery language. It has been established repeatedly that a child in full control of his language can suddenly take pleasure in reverting to the role of a baby. . . . And Gabelentz has pointed out that courting lovers quite frequently talk in child language" (Jakobson, 1968: 16–17). And again, Jakobson mentions "the coquettish, precious love-language of Russian peasant women in Northeast Siberia," consisting of replacing a /j/ for a liquid; "this so-called 'sweet-talk' is a deliberate infantilism" (ibid.). All of these are, clearly, examples of regressions of various degrees to a lowly differentiated use of phonemes. Some of the cases suggest as well that they are emotionally charged to varying degrees. However, one can attach no poetic value to these regressions.

Indeed, poetic value can be attributed, in general, only to structured regression and not to mere deliberate infantilism. Structuring, in turn, depends in one way or other on good gestalts. Regression to some undifferentiated world is mere infantilism, whereas underlying artistic pleasure we may find regression to some undifferentiated perception *by way of perceiving differentiated or intensive gestalts*. Good gestalts, or referential meaning, satisfy the Platonic censor in us so that it fails to suppress offensive, undifferentiated, or irrational information.

When discussing the relationship between poetic language and regression to a more infantile use of speech sounds, several distinctions are required. The first concerns the *kind* of regression. It may be a regression to the emotive, nonreferential use of speech sounds or to a phonological system less differentiated than that of adult language. Both kinds of regression have been discussed above. The first is characteristic of poetic language, supplying the "respectable, publicly acceptable excuse" for nonreferential use of the sound strings by way of referential use of the same sounds. The second kind (to a more primitive phonological system) is in general not characteristic of poetic language. Therefore, typically, it may be considered as no more than what Jakobson called "deliberate infantilism," even though it *may* occur in literature as the mimesis of infantile or coquettish speech.

Our second distinction will be between "mere infantilism" and regression to a relatively primitive phonological system when it is merely an optional extra to the sign nature of language. In other words, regression to a relatively primitive phonological system assumes poetic value when it occurs simultaneously with the syntagmatic, referential use of speech sounds, but forms no unambiguous part of it.

Our next distinction will be made *within* the first kind of regression, the one characteristic of poetic language. Parallel, nonreferential sound clusters, perceived by way of, and in addition to, their referential syntagmatic combination, may be either *convergent* or *divergent*. These words by Poe is an outstanding example of the former:

> . . . chilling
> And killing my Annabel Lee.

Such instances consist in repeated prominent sound clusters that converge with the stress pattern of words as well as with the poem's metric pattern; they tend to be perceived as witty or playful punning (here, *in spite of* the sad event conveyed). Divergent sound patterns, in contrast, form interwoven threads, move crisscross over relatively large areas of text, and are diffused in an unpredictable order. These sound patterns tend to be perceived more or less *unawares* and to fuse in an undifferentiated but intense musical texture characterized by an emotional quality. I have elsewhere (Tsur, 1978; 1992, chapter 4) compared at some length Poe's verse to the opening lines of Milton's *Paradise Lost* where there is a much more intense crisscross of repeated sound clusters, which usually goes unnoticed, because the clusters are perceived as some vague, unexplicable, general "musicality": they fuse in an undifferentiated background texture. This seems to be one important source of Milton's "miraculous organ voice" (for additional discussions and examples of the CONVERGENT~DIVERGENT distinction, see Tsur, 1978; 1977: 175–214, 232–38; 1983b 11–15). Here I propose to consider lines from one of the most famous French Symbolist poems, the second stanza of Baudelaire's "Correspondances":

> Comme de longs échos qui de loin se confondent
> Dans une ténébreuse et profonde unité,
> Vastes comme la nuit et comme la clarté,
> Les parfums, les couleurs et les sons se répondent.

(Like long echoes that mingle [confound] in the distance
In a dark and profound unity,
Vast as night and as the light
Perfumes, colors and sounds answer [respond] to one another.)

Henri Peyre wrote about this poem: "There is no virtuoso musical effect in the quatrains" (Burnshaw, 1964: 9). One might notice, however, that musical effects in this stanza—virtuoso or not—are extremely rich and intricate. In line 1 the sounds of *longs* are repeated in *loin*, while it "rhymes" with *sons* in line 4; it also has the nasal vowel /õ/ in common with *confondent . . . profondent . . . répondent.* The first and third words make a formally expected rhyme, while the second appears unexpectedly. The first three consonants of *profonde* reappear in *parfums*, and the first two (in a reversed order) in *répondent* (the third one in *confondent*). To these one might add *Dans une ténébreuse et profonde unité*, if we remember that /b/ is a voiced /p/. The sounds of *unité* are anticipated by *une* and echoed by *ténébreuse*, while most of its sounds are resounded in *nuit* in the next line. *Clarté*, while rhyming with *unité*, contains all the consonants of *couleur*, in the same order.

If a scholar like Peyre, who devoted a considerable part of his professional life to Baudelaire's poetry, says there is no virtuoso musical effect in this quatrain, one possible interpretation—and a very plausible one—is that he did not notice it, owing to the fusion of the sound clusters in the undifferentiated musical background texture. It should be pointed out, that most of these repetitions are sound clusters, involving two, three, or more elements. They are perceived and compared to each other; the reader, however, cannot focus his awareness on any of these strings because his attentive perception has been distracted from one string by another, so that a network of highly significant sounds has been generated, rich in effects, but only semiconsciously perceived. This diffuseness of perception is further reinforced in additional strata of the poem. The imagery suggests vague, gestalt-free, and thing-free qualities, some of them discordant, lumped together in a more or less irrational manner, also generating on the stratum of imagery a thick tissue of diffuse perceptions. On the syntactic stratum, much like the imagery the sentence has a form-blurring effect—this time it is the symmetrical stanza form that is blurred (I cannot here go into further details; the whole poem is discussed in Tsur, 1992, chapter 19). These distinctions are presented in figure 6.

In the remainder of this section I shall discuss two rare examples of

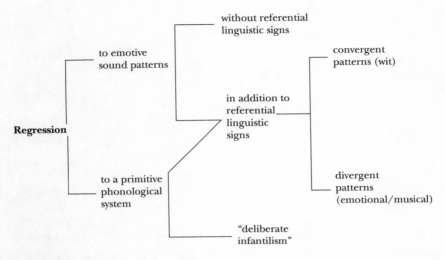

Figure 6. Phonological regressions and poetic textures.

poetry in light of this model. Let us consider first the following two lines introducing one of Hamlet's "hypermanic" outbursts (involving— if Dover Wilson is right—a pun on *solid-sullied*):

> O, that this too too solid flesh would melt,
> Thaw and resolve itself into a dew!

Kenneth Burke (1957c) proposed to base his discussion of musicality in verse on groups of "cognate" consonants (that have the same place of articulation), as shown in figure 7.

According to the first of these diagrams, the last word (*dew*) in line 2 repeats the DENTAL~ROUNDED structure of the first word (*thaw*), only it replaces the relatively recently acquired voiceless dental fricative by a voiced stop, which is a relatively early acquisition of the infant. Similarly, the middle consonant of each of the three words *solid flesh . . . melt* is /l/. *Solid* and *melt* contrast in their last consonants a voiced and a voiceless dental stop /d/~/t/, whereas *flesh* and *melt* contrast in their first consonants a labial fricative with a labial nasal, /f/~/m/; in both cases the phonemes proceed *from* the later *to* the earlier acquisition. The earlier the acquisition, the less marked the phoneme. Now consider the last three consonants of each word in *resolve itself*. The middle consonant in each triad is, again, /l/ preceded by a sibilant fricative and followed by a labial fricative. Notice also that in both positions, a voiced

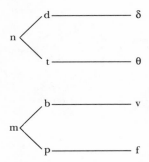

Figure 7. "Cognate" consonants.

fricative /z, v/ is replaced by its voiceless cognate /s, f/. This phrase, too, proceeds from the more to the less marked cluster of phonemes.

In these two lines, then, the reader focuses on a syntagmatic combination of phonemes used, as in any other utterance, as arbitrary linguistic entities—that is, as referential signs. Off-focus he may perceive—as, typically, in verse—certain nonreferential sound patterns that, according to our analysis, can be credited with an emotive effect. In the present instance, these sound patterns do not constitute alliteration but what Burke called "colliteration": the consonant itself is not repeated, but one of its cognates—in a similar position in the cluster. These consonant changes do observe a common direction: they proceed from the later acquired or more marked phoneme to the earlier acquired or less marked phoneme. Most of these aspects of the phoneme texture are perceived—if at all—off-focus, subliminally. How much of this has psychological reality? The fact that all changes proceed from the more differentiated to the less differentiated? Or only that they all proceed in the same direction? Or only that there is, off-focus, an intense web of muted sound repetitions? We can hardly tell.

At any rate, *if* the full extent of this process *can* be credited with psychological reality—although subliminal—a significant interplay between sound texture and semantic texture may arise. When solids melt, matter passes from a more differentiated to a less differentiated state. (It should be noted that Jakobson, when speaking of phonological regression in aphasia, occasionally resorts to such phrases as "the *dissolution* of the phonological system"). Shakespeare critics like John Middleton Murry have suggested that in Shakespeare, imagery is typically used to arouse in the reader or spectator an immediate sensation of the same idea. If the processes on which I have speculated above do have psychological reality, then the sensuous opposition *solid flesh~resolve into a dew* is subliminally reinforced on the phonological level of non-referential sound patterns, where a more differentiated phonological system is perceived as *dissolving* into a less differentiated one.

Our next example concerns the mimetic representation of "deliberate infantilism" or "love language"—but with a twist. Before turning to that example, however, let us have a fleeting look at one instance of such infantilism as it occurs in the course of the natural phonological development of infants. "MacKay cites the dialogue of a mother with her child, who months earlier had been able to produce [f] and [p] in his babbling and now asked her to 'give me my pork' (meaning *fork*); when she handed him his fork, saying in his style 'Here is your pork,' she received the answer: 'No, no! Pork! Pork!'" (Jakobson and Waugh, 1979: 159).

Similar anecdotes abound in the relevant linguistic literature. In the infant's speech, the surface realization of the phonemes [p] and [f] was not yet differentiated. This anecdote can also indicate, in relation to our discussion, how the labial fricative grows out from the bilabial stop in child language. So, in what appears to us an incidental homonym in *pork* (meaning either swine or forks) at that stage of the child's development, the child himself did discriminate two separate abstract categories behind the surface sound [p] and knew they should not be de-differentiated in adult speech.

Jakobson noted, as we have seen, that regression to a less differentiated phonological system is often charged with emotion and occurs in coquettish, precious love language, whether spontaneously or in a conventionalized manner. But not only in northwest Europe or in northeast Siberia does this precious language prevail among lovers. As one may learn from literary documents, it was prevalent (and apparently conventionalized too) in Moslem Spain in the tenth and eleventh centuries. One should not suppose that the love conventions of eleventh-century Moslem Spain had any influence on love conventions in Northeast Siberia as recorded in the twentieth century (although in both instances, liquid consonants are replaced by substitutes). It is more plausible to assume that both are founded on phonological universals with the same underlying psycholinguistic mechanism, as described in this chapter.

Let us turn to the example in which infantile regression is palpable and stylized, and the resulting quality trifling/witty. In the garden parties of eleventh-century Moslem Spain, the feasting guests occasionally made love to the "gazelles," cupbearer boys, and poets wrote love poems to them. Some of these poems recorded a coquettish sweet-talk of these boys, with a regression to an infantile phonology. These poems, as a rule, only *portrayed* this lalling talk as particularly "lovely." /r/ is one of the child's latest acquisitions; indeed, an imperfect pronunciation of /r/ was prominent in the gazelle's speech. In Arabic and classical Hebrew /g/ has a fricative allophone closely resembling the guttural /R/; it is this velar fricative /gh/ that the gazelle substitutes for the /r/. Ratsahbi (1969–70: 149) quotes a verse line by Abu Nuas, in which he expressed the excitement aroused in him by the lallation (following Ratsahbi's literal Hebrew translation) thus: "My heart melts on account of the gazelle, I desire him / the effect of the *r* in his mouth, as he articulates it"; and in another poem: "Mispronouncing the *r*, and its mispronunciation / brings about sickness and death." The poet Ibn Alzi'i describes the butler's lallation as follows: "Saying *nur* (=light) he says *nugh* with coquetry and affectation." The only Hebrew poem of this sort extant from that period, by Shemuel Hannagid, makes a structural use of this device, "yoking with violence together" two incompatible meanings that well serve the would-be lover's intention. In the poem in question, the boy's lalling results in a meaning opposite to the intended one. These are the lines in a literal translation:

> He intended to say *Raꜥ* (wrong), and said *Ghaꜥ* (touch me);
> > I approached as his tongue answered.
> He intended to say *Sura!* (away with you), and said *Sugha!*
> > (encircle me!)
> > > —So I hurried to the one encircled with
> > > > lilies.

At the end of his discussion, Ratsahbi comments: "Hannagid's portrayal of lallation . . . was superior to Alzi'i's, because he succeded in portraying the speech defects in words the meanings of which were nearly the opposite of the ones intended" (ibid., 150).

In accordance with our model we may suggest that in Alzi'i's examples no change occurs in the sign nature of language, although a phonological regression does occur. The reader is aware of the distance between the childish and adult phonology and responds—if he responds—to the charm (or affectation) of this distance. There is only one set of sounds here, the syntagmatic combination of referential signs into words, but no analogous set of nonreferential signs with their emotive effect. It is only a set of referential signs in which the phonological *signifiant* undergoes regression. Adult phonology serves here, if at all, as an unrealized potential norm. In Shəmuel Hannagid's poem, by contrast, some unexpected referential meaning is attached both to the adult and to the childish phonological norm. In this it resembles the real-life infant's use of [pork], which may signify either /pork/ (swine) or /fork/. However, in contrast to the infant's [pork], in Hannagid's poem neither meaning is left irrelevant; both are realized. Although the *signifiants* are not discriminated, the *signifiés are* discriminated, resulting in two opposite meanings. The contrast /g/~/r/ is cancelled only from the phonetic point of view, as it were, but not from the phonemic point of view. The result is a typically poetic pattern, although on a higher level of abstraction: in usual puns and ambiguities, one phonemic *signifiant* signifies two semantic *signifiés*, whereas here one phonetic *signifiant* signifies two phonemic *signifiés*, which, in turn, signify two (opposing) semantic *signifiés*.

Alternatively, we have two different phonological *signifiants*, each with its own semantic *signifié*. Each of the phonological *signifiants* may be regarded as "a sound-pattern additional to the arbitrary sign nature of language" in relation to the other. The fact that the phoneme strings /ghaᶜ/ and /sugha/ do have meanings renders the phonological regression structured. Since the patterns are convergent (rather than divergent), their perceived quality tends to be witty.

To account for this effect, we may return to Kris and Gombrich's discussion of pleasure in puns and caricatures. The pleasure they offer has two different sources. Both derive pleasure from regression to the infantile pleasures (of babbling and of inarticulate scribbling, respectively), and from the saving of mental energy by giving two things in one (for example, by calling the Christmas vacation "alcoholidays," or by representing Louis Philip as a pear). In Hannagid's example, one phonetic string gives two opposite meanings. This is achieved both by phonological regression and by using one phonetic sign-vehicle for two phonological signs that, in turn, signify two semantic entities.

"Harsh" and "Musical" Sounds

Many impressionistic comments have been made on the sound texture in language and in poetry. Some of them have been accepted for generations as indisputable truths. One aim of my theoretical work is to claim back the largest possible areas of criticism from arbitrary impressionism; at the same time, I am trying to render the reader's impression a legitimate and integral part of criticism. This twofold aim I am trying to realize in the present study too. Poetics, says Bierwisch (1970: 108), "must accept effects as given and determine the rules on which they are founded." In what follows, I shall use phonetic and phonological generalizations in an attempt to determine the rules on which certain imressionistic generalizations are founded, some widespread beliefs concerning the "aesthetic" quality of speech sounds.

My first example refers to an effect, the chief evidence for the very existence of which is anecdotal only. This anecdotal evidence, however, is so persistent and consistent that it seems to be worth the effort to try to account for it. Certain speech sounds are considered more beautiful and more musical than others. Some other sounds, on the contrary, are deemed especially ugly or unmusical. The French language, for instance, is felt to be especially musical, thanks to the nasal vowels that abound in it and to the affricates /ts/ and /pf/ that are absent from it (and which are quite conspicuous in German, for instance).

Some of the French have a feeling that nasal sounds are beautiful, whereas affricates are especially ugly. Exceptional beauty is to be found in the sound sequence [ør]. A Frenchwoman (M.A. in English and French literature) assured me on an occasion, that the word *couleur* contributes very much to the beauty of Baudelaire's "Correspondances." In saying so, she prolonged [ør] with all her French charm. All this, of course, amounts to sheer critical impressionism. I asked her, what about the sound of *puanteur* (stink)? Is it as beautiful as *couleur*? Obviously, the sound, at best, may "*seem* an echo of the sense" but have no aesthetic or referential value of its own. Yet, despite one's better judgment, one is inclined to believe that in some cases *–eur* and *-on* do have a different, possibly higher, aesthetic or expressive potential; though, again, it sounds to me as though such cases were more salient, or more frequent, in Baudelaire's or Verlaine's poetry than in Boileau's or La Fontaine's. Can such an arbitrary suggestion be somehow justified? I propose here a tentative explanation (which is in need of extensive examination). The evaluative terms for "beautiful" and "ugly" sounds can be translated into descriptive terms and even located along some more or less objective or intersubjective scale. Two sets of considerations are relevant here: first, the order of acquisition of the phonemes, and second, some acoustic cues for their perception.

The order of acquisition of phonemes has been extensively discussed here. The latest acquisitions have a double character. On the one hand, they appear to constitute the highest linguistic layer, the most rational accessories of referential language (and the first to dissolve in aphasia). On the other hand, of all the acquired phonological systems, the last acquisitions served for the longest time exclusively as gestures (onomatopoeia and interjections). In the last phases of speech-learning (and the first stages of aphasia) they may be seen as "especially charged with emotion" when used as sound gestures and, at the same time, unavailable for "arbitrary linguistic signs." So, let us quote a few passages from Jakobson relevant to the alleged beautiful or musical sounds.

> Oppositions which occur in the languages of the world comparatively rarely are among the latest phonological acquisitions of the child. Thus, the geographical distribution of nasal vowels is relatively limited, and, accordingly, these phonemes appear in French and Polish children, e.g., only after all the remaining vowels have been acquired, generally not until about the third year. (1968: 57) The number of languages with a single liquid (whether /l/ or /r/) is extraordinarily large . . . . The child has only a single liquid for a long time and acquires the other liquid only as one of his latest speech sounds. (ibid.)
> A differentiation of rounded vowels according to degree of aperture cannot arise in child language as long as the same opposition is lacking for unrounded vowels. The pair /u/~/o/ cannot, therefore, precede the pair /i/~/e/, and there are no children who have an /o/ phoneme without having acquired an /e/-phoneme. Accordingly, a number of languages have an /e/-phoneme . . ., but there is hardly any language with /o/ and not /e/. (ibid., 56)
> The vowel /ø/ does not occur in a linguistic system as long as the vowels /o/ and /e/ are not present in the same system. (ibid., 57)

These passages offer both an observational and a systematic account of the relatively late acquisition of the anecdotal "beautiful" sounds: nasal vowels and the syllable –eur. A similar story can be told for the especially "ugly" sounds. The affricates /pf/ and /ts/ are rare in the world's languages and are among the latest acquisitions of children if they occur in the mother tongue; they can be acquired only after acquisition of the respective oppositions /p/~/f/ and /t/~/s/. They frequently express disgust, contempt, or disapproval; some French find them, indeed, extremely displeasing in foreign languages and poems.

The relationship of the emotional qualities to the acoustic cues for the perception of phonemes has been extensively discussed in chapter 1;

here I shall repeat only two crucial distinctions along the [PERIODICITY] and [CONTINUITY] axes.

> *Periodicity:* The ear and brain are quick to seize upon the difference between periodic and aperiodic sounds, between tones and noises, and can detect within very close limits the moment at which periodicity begins. In normal speech, all vowel sounds, semivowels, liquids and nasals are periodic, while voiceless consonants are aperiodic. (Fry, 1970: 35)
>
> *Continuity:* The distinction between continuous and interrupted sounds—for example, between voiceless plosives and fricatives—depends on this dimension. In English the /t/ sound is most commonly characterized by a short interruption of the flow of sound, followed by noise of short duration, while /s/ is a similar noise lasting considerably longer and without interruption. (ibid., 36)

It would appear, then, that the impressionistic-subjective distinction concerning the "beauty" of some speech sounds and the "ugliness" of some others can be translated into two pairs of objective or inter-subjective opposites. First, the latest acquisitions *may* assume greater emotional or aesthetic intensity than earlier ones, for better or worse. Second, within the late acquisitions, continuous and periodic sounds are beautiful, whereas the interrupted, aperiodic sounds are ugly.

Symbolism and Nasal Vowels

It is difficult to contrive some test to verify or refute my speculations.[1] At any rate, it seems to me that if the above speculations are tolerably well-founded, they must apply not only when French poetry is compared to, for example, Hebrew or Hungarian poetry, but also when dif-

1. In phonological descriptions the French nasal vowels have been interpreted both as single phonemes and as sequences of vowel + nasal. Rohrer (1973) argues compellingly from generative phonology that in the last resort it is more parsimonious to derive the nasal vowels from sequences of vowel + nasal. This cannot affect my analysis in the present chapter. We are concerned here with a phenomenon that is basically phonetic, though in a phonological context. Rohrer himself suggests that the outcome of his derivation is a nasal vowel that is different from a sequence of vowel + nasal consonant. The psychological reality of this distinction is indicated by the fact that the split between oral and nasal consonants is one of the earliest in the infant's phonological development, whereas the nasal vowels are one of his latest acquisitions; likewise, the nasal consonants are very widespread in the languages of the world, whereas nasal vowels are among the rarest.

ferent styles within French poetry are compared. Thus, I have assumed
that a Classicist like Boileau should resort to nasal vowels in rhymes less
frequently than Symbolists like Baudelaire or Verlaine, whose poetry
strives to achieve the state of music. My findings seem to confirm this assumption. In the first one hundred lines of Boileau's *L'Art Poétique* there
are seven couplets with nasal vowels in their rhymes; in the forty lines
of Baudelaire's "Au Lecteur" (the introductory poem of *Les Fleurs du
Mal*) I found seven rhyme-pairs that contain nasal vowels (14 percent
as against 35 percent, exactly two and a half times as many). However,
nothing short of a large-scale investigation can be reliable.[2] In the remainder of this section I shall not pursue statistical phenomena but
shall closely scrutinize how the beautiful sounds actually work in a few
notorious instances of Symbolist poetry.

It seems that the subjective ugly affricates and beautiful nasal vowels and the sound sequence *–eur* can be translated into the objective
oppositions [±CONTINUOUS] and [±PERIODIC]—amplified in phonemes
of late acquisition. The later acquisitions *may* have greater emotional
impact than the earlier ones. Generally, neither in everyday nor in literary language is this difference perceptible. The referential meaning,
and even some of the more outstanding phonetic aspects, "usurp" the
reader's attention so that such subtle oppositions are subdued or completely ignored. These phenomena can contribute—if at all—to poetry
only when the reader is able (using Keats's phrase) "to make up his mind
about nothing—to let the mind be a thoroughfare for all thoughts,"
sensations and impressions, "without any irritable reaching after fact
and reason" or articulate shapes; in short, in impressionistic, divergent,
gestalt-free poetry, such as the second stanza of Baudelaire's "Correspondances" (discussed above), or Verlaine's "Chanson d'Automne":

> Les sanglots longs
> Des violons
> De l'automne
> Blessent mon coeur
> D'une langueur
> Monotone.

2. This distribution, of course, is not fixed throughout Baudelaire's poetry. In the next
few poems in "Bénédiction" and "Les Phares" the percentage is somewhat lower, whereas
in the sonnet "Correspondances" there are three rhyme-pairs involving nasal vowels
(almost 43 percent). But in all cases, the percentages were considerably higher than in
Boileau's poem.

Tout suffoquant
Et blême, quand
Sonne l'heure,
Je me souviens
Des jours anciens
Et je pleure.

Et je m'en vais
Au vent mauvais
Qui m'emporte,
De çà, de là,
Pareil à la
Feuille Morte.

The first stanza of this poem has often been quoted as a typical, or rather an outstanding, representative of Symbolism. In Symbolism, the contours

> become vague and dissolve into infinity. It is not the conceptual meaning of words that counts, but rather their aura, their mood, the mysterious feelings they arouse. They do not represent, do not theorize, do not *tell* things, but aim at evocative effects. One need not understand their poems, but feel them, live them. . . . This poem does not appeal to understanding: "The long sobbings of Autumn's violins wound my heart with a monotonous languor." The image—not intended for the eyes—*qua* image, isn't even very interesting—but with the music of the poem, together with the mood of words, it is full of omen, lilting, sorrowful, deathly. It is impossible to translate such a poem. (Szerb, 1943: III, 143)

I am not going to demonstrate how Szerb's generalization works on the semantic level (although it is worth noting that the only stable objects in the poem are the dead leaves carried about by the wind, the rest is gestalt-free and thing-free; Autumn's violins are mentioned for the sake of their sound, not shape). I shall take this passage only as evidence that it is sometimes (or always) perceived as if the aura, the mood of words, the mysterious feeling aroused by them, counted rather than their conceptual meaning.

The first thing to note about the poem's sound structure is that *all* the rhymes of the first two stanzas are based on "beautiful" sounds, either nasal vowels, or the sound sequence –*eur*. The only deviation is because of the feminine ending at the middle and end of the first stanza. One of Verlaine's ways of introducing movement and a sense of alteration into the phonetic structure of these stanzas is that in the first one he manipulates a nasal rhyme into the feminine ending, and in the second one he manipulates an *–eur* rhyme. In the former, the feminine ending is bound to turn the nasal vowel (of, for example, *monoton*) into a nasal consonant. Nasal consonants, however, still share certain acoustic features with nasal vowels, such as nasality, periodicity, and relatively low encodedness. So, in the present context they may support the musical and emotional qualities of the nasal vowels.

On the poem's prosodic structure, contributing to its divergent effect, I want to make these observations. Since French meter is syllabic, Verlaine does not have, say, Milton's option of divergent prosodic structures. In this poem stress pattern cannot diverge from metric pattern. Therefore he resorted to a different device for weakening the prosodic shape of his verse: he did away with the dodecasyllabic verse lines divided into two symmetrical halves (remember his precept: "De la musique avant toute chose, / Et pour cela préfère l'Impair"). In the present poem, an endecasyllabic unit is substituted for the symmetrical alexandrine, broken up into three lines consisting of 4+4+3 syllables (followed by a feminine ending). So, in spite of the stanza's overall symmetry, irregularity rather than regularity is emphasized in its prosodic structure. The single clause running through it is thus broken up into six perceptual units. The more we emphasize the continuity of the unit, the more backgrounded are the prosodic units, and the rhyming sounds fuse into the background texture. The more clearly articulated the line endings, the more clearly the sound patterns that constitute the rhyme scheme stand out.

One of the poem's significant prosodic characteristics relates to the psycholinguistic mechanisms of spoonerisms and slips of the tongue. It can be observed in the first and last stanzas. First, the last syllable in the first line [lõ], with the feature [+NASAL] in its vowel, is preceded by the same syllable, with the oral counterpart of the vowel in it [lo]; the feature [+NASAL] has been transferred from this vowel to the preceding syllable in the same word [sã]. Second, in the last stanza we have another poetic spoonerism: *Vent* in line 2 repeats "m'en" in line 1; only the first sounds of the two successive words have been interchanged: "Et je *m*'en **v**ais / Au **v**ent *m*auvais." It is, in fact, only the features [+NASAL] and [+FRICATIVE] that have been interchanged in these two labial consonants. In this way, the diffuse quality of the sound texture is actively enhanced at these points of the poem so that not only the sound structure of words but the structure of phonemes is felt to be diffuse, in a flux. Moreover, this sudden shift of features consists in a sudden shift of mental sets that is typical in intense emotional and witty responses.

The skeptical reader may suspect that such shifts of distinctive features, as in these cases the shift of nasality or its interchange with [+FRICATIVE], may reflect my own ingenuity rather than linguistic processes that have psychological reality. However, Victoria Fromkin's linguistic study (1973) of the slips of the tongue phenomenon brought to light a wealth of evidence concerning the psychological reality of a great variety of linguistic rules. An interesting aspect of the more than 6,000 speech errors she collected, involving substitution and permutation of various sound segments, concerned the type of speech units affected. What is important is that even individual features may be exchanged, as in "glear plue sky" for "clear blue sky," where the feature [+VOICED] is transferred from the initial phoneme of "blue" to the initial phoneme of "clear." "When a person says *cedars of Lemadon* instead of *cedars of Lebanon*, the nasality features of the [b] and the [n] are reversed. The intended oral labial [b] becomes a nasal labial [m] and the intended nasal alveolar [n] an oral alveolar [d]" (ibid., 114). Fromkin's point is that such errors demonstrate that the units of language developed by linguists are real units with an independent existence in the mental grammar. For our purpose, the point is that in Verlaine's poem the transfer of the feature nasality not only has psychological reality but makes the sound texture less compact with the help of a deep-seated, subliminal process that escapes conscious introspection. It should be noticed, however, that in "Lemadon" the shift of the feature [NASALITY] results in a nonsense word, whereas in Verlaine's poem both words occur together and yield a meaningful phrase (see our discussion of Shəmuel Hannagid's poem above).

We have devoted some consideration, both structurally and statistically, to the relationship between French Symbolism and nasal vowels. We have found a rather significant numerical difference between the sound structure of seventeenth-century French Classicism and nineteenth-century French Symbolism. And we have accounted for it in terms of a model based on the child's acquisition of the phonological system of his mother tongue, as propounded in this chapter. I would like to add an explanation based on the cognitive strategies expounded in the first chapter. There we distinguished a speech mode and a nonspeech mode of auditory perception. In the latter mode, precategorical sensory information is restructured (recoded) so that a phonetic category rather than precategorical sensory information reaches consciousness. Voiceless plosives are more thoroughly restructured than vowels or sonorant consonants; that is, in the latter, more precategorical sensory information reaches consciousness than in the former. I have suggested that there may be a third poetic mode in which the precategorical sensory information that reaches consciousness becomes somehow significant. Crowder and Morton have found that in certain orally (but not visually) presented memory tasks there is a certain recency effect where the crucial speech sounds are vowels, but not voiceless plosives. They suggested that the explanation of this effect was, that the rich precategorical auditory information lingered on in echoic memory where the relatively less thoroughly restructured vowels were concerned, whereas in the more thoroughly restructured voiceless stops little or no such information was accessible. Crowder later found that this recency effect could be drastically reduced by a "verbal suffix," that is, when a nonsense syllable such as /ba/ was used to indicate when the recall attempt was to be started, but not when a pure tone was used. Each later arrival, they explained, exerted "lateral inhibition" on earlier arrivals in the neurological system so that the abstract phonetic category should linger on, but not the precategorical sensory information. In relation to the *rumble—Drum* sound pattern in a stanza by FitzGerald, I suggested that the auditory trace may be enhanced rather than inhibited when several conditions meet, such as (1) when the sounds involved are continuous and periodical; (2) when massive sound clusters are repeated; (3) when semantic features of the words tend to draw attention *to*, rather than *away from*, the acoustic and articulatory features of sound patterns; (4) when one of the syllables concerned is the last one in a perceptual unit (that is, no verbal suffix follows it).

A second relevant issue is Repp's discovery of the cognitive strategies to attend at will to the abstract phonetic categories of the fricative sibilants [s, š], or switch to the underlying precategorical auditory information. "The skill involved lay in perceptually segregating the noise from its vocalic context, which then made it possible to attend to its 'pitch.' Without this segregation, the phonetic percept was dominant." (See chapter 1, "Acoustic Coding.")

Now, do we have reasons to assume that a similar skill is involved in our ability to attend to the auditory information underlying nasal vowels? At least one anecdote suggests a positive answer. The other day an old friend of mine dropped in when I was busy with this manuscript. This friend was likely to make a "theoretically naive informant" with a more than usually keen poetic intuition. When she asked me what I was doing, I explained: "Consider the words *Ping* and *Pong*: which one is darker?" After a few minutes' silence she answered, as expected, "Pong." But she added: "This demonstration is not valid because I cheated: during the silence I was repeating, and listening to, *Pinnng* and *Ponnng*," and saying so she unnaturally prolonged the nasalized portion of the vowels. What she thought was cheating was in fact the cognitive strategy, or "skill," of prolonging and segregating that portion of the word's sound structure most easily accessible to introspection.

Just after writing that paragraph, Rakerd's (1984) article reached me, where he adduces carefully controlled experimental evidence that vowels in consonantal context are perceived more linguistically than are isolated vowels. One possible explanation is that such vowels are subject to "parallel transmission" (see chapter 1); in other words, "the talker often coarticulates the neighboring segments of an utterance (that is, overlaps their productions) such that the acoustic signal is jointly influenced by those segments" (123). One of Rakerd's major findings strongly suggests that the difference between the two modes is not based on what the perceiver *knows* must be the case but on his perceiving something in the stimulus: "the consonantal influence in perception had more to do with stimulus-based factors than with knowledge-based factors" (ibid., 133). Moreover, "with isolated vowels listeners attended in a piecewise manner to three different vowel dimensions in a way that was more consistent with other aspects of linguistic behavior" (ibid., 1134).

These findings, although consistent with my previous speculations, provide no unambiguous proof for them. Rakerd produced evidence that his subjects isolated and perceived distinctive features in the sound stimulus, but did not produce, nor did he look for, evidence that they perceived precategorical auditory information. At any rate, he did produce convincing evidence in carefully controlled laboratory conditions that the cognitive strategy to perceive *subcategorical* elements in vowels was to segregate them from their consonantal context.

I suggest, then, that when we perform a poem like Verlaine's "Chanson d'Automne," we choose from the beginning a delivery style that would allow us a sufficient margin of freedom to manipulate the nasal back vowels subliminally prolonging and segregating their crucial portions so as to allow us to perceive and register their dark quality, as well as their rich sonorous quality, before "lateral inhibition" by later arrivals may occur; or so as to proactivate and enhance the sound trace of similar sound patterns to arrive later; or, at least, to pronounce the nasal vowels in such a way that a sufficiently perceptible portion of their acoustic signal not jointly influenced by neighboring segments should remain. This margin of freedom is not easy to achieve. It seems to be possible only in a general state of mind in which parallel cognitive processing is encouraged, whereas in connected speech there is a tendency to proceed linearly rather than move in different directions from the central sequence. As I have suggested, in poetry one may distinguish a convergent from a divergent style. In the latter, perceptual and conceptual gestalts are considerably weaker than in the former. To allow for the disruption—though subliminal—of the linear sequencing of speech sounds (that is, for segregating the relevant portions of the auditory stream), the whole message must be less thoroughly organized on all levels as the linguistic stress pattern diverges from the conventional metric pattern, and as does the syntactic unit (clause, sentence) from the prosodic unit (line). In the world stratum of divergent poems we frequently find diffuse, shape-free (and sometimes thing-free) entities rather than things that have stable characteristic visual shapes. In short, the freedom to adopt the cognitive strategy of segregating or integrating the crucial portions of the sound stream, so as to move back and forth between auditory and phonetic modes of listening, is at its fullest when the cognitive system on all levels of the poem is not under the control of some strong shape, definite direction, or patent purpose. In such a context, the greater the divergence of the repeated sound clusters from strings of arbitrary verbal signs, the more they assume the emotive effects of nonreferential sound gestures.

We have seen at the beginning of this section that in Baudelaire's "Au Lecteur" there is a considerably greater proportion of nasal-vowel rhymes than in Boileau's *L'Art Poétique*. To keep things in proportion, I wish to remark that the nasal vowels in this poem are perceived as far less active than, say, in "Chanson d'Automne." One conspicuous reason for this seems to be that the materials handled by the poem are far from thing-free and gestalt-free. Much of the imagery is based on things that have stable characteristic visual shapes. The basic attitude of the poem is to *persuade*, so it exhibits the psychological atmosphere of definite direction and patent purpose. As a result, the cognitive system *is* under the control of good gestalts on several levels, and the sounds that are potentially charged with emotions are felt to be perceived as abstract categories rather than auditory information. As this example may indicate, the Symbolist poets seemed to have a predilection for emotionally active speech sounds in prominent positions. However, in this poem the potential sensuous and emotional activity of these sounds is kept down because they are placed in a context of things, shapes, and a psychological atmosphere of definite direction, patent purpose, and a sense of control.

A further comment is pertinent. I have suggested that the first stanza of "Chanson d'Automne" strives to achieve the state of music. Here, the highly active, emotionally charged sound texture is also fused in an imagery that forms a gestalt-free and thing-free, diffuse semantic texture. In such a context, the poem's musical nature is enhanced by the fact that the dominant speech sounds in the stanza are, like the sounds of music, continuous and periodic.

Nasal vowels, then, entertain a special status in poetic language: they have exceptionally great emotional effectiveness. This is the reason that both Symbolist and "hypnotic" poetry have a predilection for them. I have pointed out a variety of sources for this exceptional emotional appeal. First of all, nasal vowels are relatively unencoded; their rich precategorical sensory information becomes available to the reader or listener. Second, this precategorical sensory information is periodic, and thus nasal vowels approximate, within the boundaries of linguistic reference, the state of music—a pleasurable experience toward which Symbolist poetry aspired. Third, nasal vowels are relatively late additions to the child's phonological system, which, according to our analysis, amplifies their emotional appeal. Fourth, as recent phonetic research has shown, "the spectra of nasalized vowels are acoustically less distinct" (Wright, 1986: 47). The psychological validity of this finding has been supported by experimental phonology, which points out a loss of contrast among the members of the nasalized set, as one of the perceptual consequences of nasalization (ibid., 55). "If vowel nasalization be expected to distribute energy more evenly through the spectrum by lowering the amplitude of the oral formants . . . and by introducing additional spectral prominences, the factor scores should shift towards zero, thereby centralizing the nasalized vowels and reducing contrast" (ibid., 60). It should be noticed that whereas neoclassicists like Boileau (or Alexander Pope) had an inclination toward clear-cut, polarized, symmetrical contrasts in their poetry, the kind of Symbolist poetry we are talking about (Baudelaire, Verlaine) tends to avoid sharp contrasts and to cherish fine, gradual shadings, resulting in "chaotic overdifferentiation" in the perception of the world; this may constitute cognitive overload on the reader's system, which he may tend to handle by collapsing it in a thick, lowly differentiated texture. In this context, Wright's analysis may imply that nasal vowels too (so prominent in Baudelaire's and Verlaine's poetry) would modestly contribute to this chaotic overdifferentiation (this cognitive overload) resulting from the avoidance of sharp contrasts.

We have encountered Szerb's claim that it is impossible to translate the first stanza of "Chanson d'Automne." It should be noted, however, that any poetry is impossible to translate. It is always a miracle when a translation is successful—a miracle that sometimes *does* happen to poets. I agree, notwithstanding, that with such poems as this one, the miracle can be expected to happen less often. In the meantime, the model of phonological universals put forward in this chapter may help—if not to predict—to account for the preference of sounds *after the event* in the translation of a poem like "Chanson d'Automne." Consider, for instance, a language such as Hebrew that has no nasal vowels or an /ø/. What speech sounds would a poet seek out as the emotional and musical equivalents of the sounds of Verlaine's poem? Let us have a look at Jabotinsky's Hebrew translation of the poem's first stanza.

> Binhi mamror
> Homɛ kinor
> Tevet paruᶜa,
> Vəʾɛl halev
> Ḥoder kəʾev
> Vəgaᶜaguᶜa.

Jabotinsky attempted to compensate in his translation for the lack of nasal vowels and /ø/ in his target language by using as many sonorants and back vowels as possible, manipulating them into as prominent places as possible. As we have seen in this chapter, rounded back vowels are later acquisitions of the child than the unrounded front vowels, and thus they are more emotionally charged or more musical in the appropriate circumstances.[3] In the first two lines there is only one voiceless plosive, /k/, and one voiced plosive, /b/. Of the periodic consonants, /r/ is the latest acquisition of the young child, so it occurs in this transla-

---

3. This explanation may perhaps be supplemented by Fónagy's findings (discussed at length in chapter 1) concerning the correlations between back vowels and tender emotions or dark colors.

tion after the oral vowel /o/, replacing as it were nasalization (occurring three times in two rhyme-syllables).

Of the earlier acquisitions, the periodic sonorants occur—/m/ three times and /n/ twice—in the first two lines, thus setting the poem's musical-emotional tone. In other words, Jabotinsky attempted to render the sound texture of the first two lines as sonorous, as dark, and of as late acquisition as possible, and to manipulate as many of these features as he possibly could into the rhyme. His expressive use of the /r/ is especially noteworthy (though by no means rare in poetry). Many poets and lay readers of poetry have perceived in the /r/ a hard, menacing quality. This quality is derived, according to Fónagy (1971: 161; 1983: 95–103), from the phallic nature of the "strong erection of the tongue" in its pronunciation. "This apical *r* is significantly more frequent in aggressive and erotic poems than in idyllic poems by the same authors." In this instance, however, a different potential of the /r/ has been exploited: the sonority of the rich precategorical auditory information accessible to consciousness in a continuous consonant that has a relatively great emotive potential for sound gestures, being a relatively late acquisition of the child (see chapter 5).

Most of the sounds not predicted by our model, or predicted to be comparatively *rare* in the translation (such as the three voiceless plosives in the third line), are to be attributed to a compromise between the conflicting stringencies of the phonetic and semantic features required in the present context (semantic and phonetic features are available in natural language in a combination that is typically different from the requirements of this—or, in fact, any—poem).

The Hungarian translator may consider himself luckier. First of all, /ø/ *is* available to him; what is more, he can hardly avoid it because it occurs in the Hungarian word for "Autumn": *ősz*. Nasalized vowels are available in Hungarian, although less readily than in French, in a few root words, and most notably in the frequentative suffix –*ong*. Hungarian Symbolist poets, presumably under the influence of French Symbolism, made sometimes marked efforts as a special tour de force to achieve musical effects based on nasal (back) vowels. And one such outstanding instance is Árpád Tóth's brilliant translation of "Chanson d'Automne":

> Ősz húrja zsong,
> Jajong, busong
> A tájon,

S ont monoton
Bút konokon
És fájón.

The translator's preference for nasal vowels and consonants is conspicuous. I shall note only that the Hungarian word for "its violin"
(*hegedűje*) has been replaced by a metonymy, *húrja* (its string), introducing a dark back vowel (/u/) and a sonorant (/r/), as well as eliminating,
by the same token, such plosives as the /g/ and /d/ of the proper term.[4]
  Encouraged by the Hungarian translator's feast of nasality, I attempted several years ago to render lines 4–6 in Hebrew, as follows:

Yanʿim yagon
ʿAmum hagon
Vəgaʿguʿa.
(Sounds monotonous sorrow and yearning).

These words make ample use of dark back vowels and nasal consonants as well as the velar stop [g] and the glottal stop [ʿ] in close
proximity. Nonetheless, the poem refused to assume a musical quality
comparable to the French original or Tóth's Hungarian translation.
This was most conspicuous precisely where I expected the greatest
similarity, in the rhyme words *yagon-hagon*. At that time I could describe the difference only in an intuitive fashion: the *–gon* sequence
in the Hebrew rhyme sounded somehow too decisive, too conclusive,
too assertive, too solid compared to the corresponding sequences in

4. It should be remembered that we are *prophesying after the event,* and one should not rule
out finding a complete failure to produce any sort of equivalent of the musical texture,
except for the elementary rhyme scheme and, perhaps, some target language equivalent
of the original meter. Such an illustrious failure is Lőrinc Szabó's Hungarian translation
of the same stanza:

  Zokog, zokog
  az ősz konok
  hegedűje,
  zordúl szivem,
  fordúl szivem
  keserűre.

To be sure, Szabó too was a great translator (who, among other things, had collaborated
with Babits and Tóth on a full Hungarian translation of *Les Fleurs du Mal*), but not for
this kind of poetry, which demands intense musicality and relaxation of the control of
shapes.

French or Hungarian. Phonetically and phonologically speaking, in French we are dealing with nasal vowels proper, whereas in Hungarian we are confronted with an allophone of the oral vowel, strongly nasalized by coarticulation with the subsequent nasal consonant. In Hebrew, by contrast, the nasalizing effect of coarticulation is barely existent, or becomes barely perceptible (as will be apparent in a moment, the latter rather than the former may be the case). Haruko Kawasaki's work in experimental phonology throws interesting light on the aesthetic repercussions of this difference between Hebrew and Hungarian. "It has been well documented that . . . nondistinctive nasalization has a physiological cause: lowering of the velum adjacent to nasal consonants" (1986: 86). Historically, many instances of nasal vowels are derived from such allophonic nasalization, when the nasal consonant is dropped, as for instance French /sã/ (*cent* = "hundred") from Latin *centum*. The acoustic perturbation of the oral vowel by the subsequent nasal stop "may be taken for granted and factored out of the phonetic percept constructed for a word, as long as the segment responsible for the perturbation is detected" (ibid., 87). "This . . . is what permits nondistinctive, that is, allophonic, nasalization on vowels next to nasal consonants. If the perturbing segment is not detected, for whatever reason, then the perturbation is not expected and is not factored out; it is then included as part of the phonetic percept of the word" (ibid.). This, she claims, is a phonological universal, and she brings supporting evidence from a large variety of languages with a wide range of phonological constraints in them. "A testable consequence of this hypothesis is that nasalization on a vowel should be perceptually more evident as adjacent nasal consonants become attenuated, for it is the presence of the nasal consonant that permits listeners to reconstruct the orality of a vowel and its absence or weakness which permits the nasalization to be heard" (ibid.).

In two experiments she adduces evidence that strongly (though not conclusively) suggests that this may indeed be the case. In these experiments, the amplitude of nasal consonants in nonsense syllables was attenuated in five steps. The stimuli were presented to experimental subjects on two occasions. In the first run they were asked to indicate whether they heard nasal consonants in the stimuli. In the second run they judged the degree of nasality of the vowel. "It is safe to conclude from the experiments using two different methods of psychological rating that, as predicted, the degree of perceived nasality of a vowel is enhanced by the attenuation of adjacent nasal consonants or, conversely, is reduced by the presence of adjacent nasal consonants" (ibid., 94).

Compare the name of the German philosopher *Kant* to the British pronunciation of the contraction *can't*. They can be treated as almost a minimal pair. One of the most obtrusive differences between them concerns precisely the issue discussed here: in *Kant* the nasal consonant [n] has its full, solid body; accordingly, no or little nasalization is perceived in the preceding vowel. In *can't*, by contrast, the [n] is strongly attenuated by coarticulation with the [t]; accordingly, a strong nasal quality is perceived in the preceding vowel. Likewise, in Hungarian *zsong* (or, for that matter, in English *song*) the voiced velar stop [g] drastically attenuates the adjacent [n] (both being produced by manipulation of the velum); by the same token, the nasal "perturbation" in the preceding oral vowel becomes palpable. In Hebrew *yagon* and *hagon*, by contrast, no such attenuation takes place in the nasal consonant; correspondingly, no nasal perturbation becomes perceptible in the preceding vowel. The nasal perturbation in Hungarian *zsong* (or in English *song*) is perceived as diffuse but rich precategorical sensory information that increases "chaotic overdifferentiation"; whereas the "weak, residual" [n] is perceived as a diffuse, vague, and evasive category rather than a compact phonetic one. In this way, the perceptual contrast between the vowel and the consonant is also reduced. All this may reinforce the emotional atmosphere typically cherished by Symbolist poetry. In Hebrew no such attenuation of nasal consonants takes place; so, the Hebrew translator of Verlaine must be content with fully realized, relatively compact nasals.

Another notorious instance of the exploitation of nasal vowels in Hungarian poetry is the following stanza from Mihály Babits's "Sad Poem":

> Barangoló, borongó,
> Ki bamba bún borong,
> Borzongó bús bolyongó
> Baráttalan bolond.
> (A straying, gloomy [person],
> Brooding over stolid sorrow,
> A shuddering, mournful, roaming,
> Friendless fool.)

This poem became notorious for its alliteration: ten of its eleven words begin with a *b*, without violating the natural word order (or, for that matter, the rhyme pattern or the iambic meter). While in Verlaine's poem one may make out a good case for onomatopoeia or for an expressive sound pattern, many readers have difficulties in their attempt to account for the strong emotional impact of the sound effect in this stanza. Fónagy (1971: 169) writes: "According to the results of experiments made with Hungarian readers, within this context . . . , the voiced stop suggested mainly two images: nine readers out of twenty heard a bell sounding or saw a solitary bell-tower, while six others were reminded of the mournful sound of funeral drums." We have no indication of the literary sophistication of Fónagy's subjects; nor do we know what was the exact question to which these answers were given. At any rate, I do not think this is the most illuminating way to handle the stanza's sound effect. Neither the bells nor the funeral drums are mentioned in any way in this stanza or anywhere else in the poem. These subjects' responses have introduced irrelevant images and "noisy" elements into the stanza, which, I submit, only distract attention from the real sources of its patent emotional effect. In the first place, it would appear that the dominant emotional effect in the sound stratum is set by the overwhelming abundance of nasal back vowels (rather than by alliterating voiced stops). As I shall try to show, the bell or drum images, too, are more likely to be suggested by the nasal back vowels than by the voiced stops. The voiced stops seem to have here, at most, a corroborating effect.

It would appear that the theory propounded in this study may supply a more straightforward explanation of the emotional impact of this stanza's sound effect. It seems to draw on the cumulative effect of several factors. First, we have an intensive set of nonreferential sound patterns superimposed on the arbitrary, referential linguistic signs. This, as I suggested earlier in this chapter, may have a marked emotional effect. Second, nasal vowels are relatively rare in the world's languages and are of the infants' latest acquisitions within the vowel system of those languages in which they occur. From this, it follows that they serve in babbling until a relatively late stage and are especially loaded with emotion; they are especially prone to serve as sound gestures: emotive sound patterns or onomatopoeia. Third, all vowels, as well as the sonorants /l, r, m, n/ that relatively abound in this stanza, are continuous, periodic, lowly encoded speech sounds and thus tend to contribute, in the proper circumstances, to the perceived effect of some tender emotion (as suggested in Chapter 1). It is in this phonetic context that the periodic aspect of the [+VOICED] feature of the voiced stop /b/ and the voiced fricative /z/ is also emphasized. Fourth, as suggested in chapter 1, back vowels, whose F_1 and F_2 are not easily differentiated, may add in the proper thematic circumstances a dark tint to the tender emotional quality of a poem.

The foregoing analysis highlights the possible dangers of relying on the responses of subjects in an experimental investigation into the sound effects of poetry. If one relies on subjects of high theoretical sophistication, one may not expect them to produce unbiased responses. If, on the other hand, one is relying on relatively naive subjects, one may not expect them to use sufficiently sophisticated tools needed for describing and locating the source of the perceived emotional effects of the sounds. Being immensely aware of the emotional impact of the sound structure of this stanza, they may have had recourse to the relatively crude tools that may have been at their disposal. Rather than being free from bias, they seem to have been biased by an inadequate theory of sound effects.[5]

Having subliminally perceived, beyond the phonetic categories, some rich precategorical periodic information, they projected some musical instrument (bell or drum) onto the stanza to establish some onomatopoetic relationship between the stanza's sound structure and the sounds of the musical instruments. These instruments, in turn, are conceived as part of a stereotypically mournful situation (funeral), the mournfulness of which is felt to reinforce the stanza's sadness. My claim is that the theory propounded here may account for the emotional effect felt by many readers to exist in this stanza's sound structure in a way that is systematic as well as more parsimonious, that does not have to rely on the introduction of more or less arbitrary images into the poem.

Referentiality, Serial Position, and Milton's "Miraculous Organ Voice"

Finally, let me return to the suggestion "that in poetic language speech sounds are used as 'arbitrary linguistic signs,' combined into

5. In chapter 1, I quoted Hrushovsky (1980), who distinguishes four types of sound patterns in poetry: onomatopoeia (mimetic), expressive, focusing, and neutral. A subject who is aware of the first possibility only is likely to go to great lengths to produce mimetic associations when asked to account for the effects of sound in poetry. So, when asked to account for the relation of the poem's sound patterns to its emotional quality, Fónagy's subjects could think, presumably, of nothing better than of the imitation of some mournful instrument. This is, I believe, the only lesson to be learned from the associations

words by a 'syntagmatic' relationship, forming entities of linguistic value; at the same time, there is a nonreferential combination of the same sounds, based on repetition, forming reference-free qualities, exploiting not so much differentiated contrastive features, as similarities." There seems to be, indeed, some evidence that the two kinds of sound patterns are processed in different ways at *some* level of cognitive organization. Roger Brown in his psycholinguistic study of the Tip-of-the-Tongue Phenomenon found that subjects who had a word "at the tip of the tongue" but could not recall it could nevertheless produce a large amount of information about it, among other things *similar sound* (ss) words and *similar meaning* (sm) words. "Generic recall of the *partial* variety is evidenced by the subjects' knowledge of letters in the target word. This knowledge shows a bowed serial-position effect since it is better for the ends of a word than for the middle and somewhat better for beginning positions than for final positions" (Brown, 1970: 291). The accuracy of the recall of letters was tested for the following positions: first, second, third, third-last, second-last, and last. "The ss curve is at all points above the sm curve. . . . The values for the last three positions of the ss curve quite closely match the values for the first three positions. The values for the last three positions of the sm curve, on the other hand, are well above the values of the first three positions. Consequently, the *relative* superiority of the ss curve is greater in the first three positions" (ibid., 286–87). One should not be surprised that words deliberately provided for their similar sounds are more similar to the target word than words provided for their similar meanings. It seems, however, to be significant that accuracy is *relatively* better at the beginning for ss words and relatively better at the end for sm words.

A later experiment with listening to and recalling monosyllabic words in a noise-masked condition shows a smaller number of errors in the final position than in the initial position (Brady et al., 1982: 350). The uneven distribution of errors across the positions seems to correspond with the relative acoustic saliency of the segments. The results of research on the speech cues suggest that the consonant in the final position is more clearly represented in the acoustic signal than is the initial consonant. "Syllable final formants have been observed to have transitions of greater duration . . . and greater frequency change than have initial transitions. . . . Thus final consonants may be easier to

---

reported. In this respect, Pope's aphorism seems to be very much to the point: "A little learning is a dangerous thing."

perceive because a greater amount of information specifies their identity" (ibid., 359). If further data confirm this tendency, it may explain certain observed facts and qualities in poetry. Thus, one prominent feature of Milton's "miraculous organ voice" is an obtrusive effect of 'powerful' consonants in some passages of the strongest musical impact. The consonant clusters, not necessarily repetitive, impinge themselves on one's perception more powerfully than, for example, in Spenser. A consonant count in these passages reveals a slightly greater number of consonants in Milton's iambic pentameter lines than in those of some other poets. This numerical difference is too small to account for the compelling perceptual difference. Oras (1957), however, found a significant difference between the position of consonant strings in stressed syllables in Milton and Spenser. Milton typically resorts to monosyllabics like *earth, arms, Heav'ns, world, rowld, hunt.* Spenser's strings of consonants typically occur at the onset of stressed syllables, as in *prey, stray, bray, speed, steed, smoke, stroke* (12). If it is true that when attention is focused on the meaning of words, more information is allocated to the final phonemes, then Milton's consonant strings are bound to be more obtrusive on one's attention. This effect may be heightened by the interaction of gestalt-free elements in divergent poetry, as Milton's, where the number of run-on lines and thing-free qualities is much greater than in Spenser's convergent poetry. As I have shown elsewhere in great detail, Milton is one of the most divergent of the major English poets, whereas Spenser is one of the most convergent, with greater metric regularity than even Pope (see, for example, Tsur, 1977: 56–61; 76–82, 180–89). Thus, a general state of mind is achieved in which parallel cognitive processing is encouraged, as suggested above, with a sufficient margin of freedom to manipulate the relevant speech sounds, subliminally prolonging and segregating their crucial portions.

If we consider the implications of the serial-position effect for the issue of acoustic information somehow reverberating in the reader's or listener's acoustic memory in certain poetic structures, they seem to be a mixed blessing. On the one hand, they corroborate the possibility that "pure," reference-free speech sounds receive different cognitive processing than speech sounds that serve as "arbitrary linguistic signs" in referential language. On the other hand, by combining Brown's and Oras's findings with my own observations concerning poetic language, one would expect to find this co-occurrence: perceived musical richness + reference-free sound-patterns + *initial* (rather than final) consonant strings. One would expect to encounter such a configuration in Milton's "miraculous organ voice" rather than in Spenser's fairly single-minded, convergent rhythms. In other words, one would expect to find the consonant strings in initial position in Milton's rather than in Spenser's poetry.

Perhaps a reasonable explanation would run as follows. The accuracy for the last three positions in Brown's findings was high for both ss and sm words; thus, poetry that makes intensive use of both referential and nonreferential sound patterns should be expected to focus attention on *final* positions. By the same token, this attention coincides with focusing on that part of the word where the phonetic information is richer (according to Brady et al., 1983). Furthermore, according to some of the foregoing speculations, the weaker gestalts (both on the sound and the represented world stratum) in Milton's poetry make it more possible to attend to the rich precategorical auditory information then the much stronger gestalts in Spenser's poetry. If all this is true, then Spenser's poetry with its initial consonant strings *distracts* attention from precisely that part of the word where the greatest sensory richness could be perceived.

Coda: Word Order and Processing Effort

Finally, in light of these findings and analyses I would like to revisit an issue discussed in the section "Thought-Experiment with 'Dark Vowels'" in chapter 1. There I discussed reduplications like *criscross* or *Ping-Pong* in which it is more natural for the darker back vowel to come last. I suggested that this was a specific instance of the principle that in a sequence of two or more coordinate items, it is most natural for the one that requires the greatest processing effort to come last. In a brilliant article called "Word Order," Cooper and Ross (1975) make similar observations on "the ordering of certain conjoined elements." The scope of the *kinds* of ordering principles and range of examples in this essay go far beyond the issues discussed in this work. On the other hand, the kinds of cognitive explanations they briefly suggest in the sections "Psychological Evidence" and "Conclusions" are very much in the spirit of the explanations offered here. And so is the principle they offer as the overall explanation: "Frozen conjuncts which are easier to process tend to occupy place 1 in a freeze, enabling the listener to handle the preliminary processing of this conjunct while new information is still being presented to him by the speaker" (ibid., 92).

In the section relevant to us, they describe the sequence of vowels in a freeze (frozen conjunct) as a subsequence of the sequence of vowels that roughly corresponds to the vowels in figure 2 of chapter 1, with reference to F_2. "As Morris Halle has pointed out to us, this sequence can be defined acoustically by a monotonic decrease in the second formant frequency" (ibid., 73). In chapter 1, I described the same sequence as consisting in decreasing distance between F_1 and F_2. I suggested there that to save mental processing space, the member that requires greater processing effort is deferred to the end; and the nearer the formants to one another, the more difficult it is to perceptually discriminate them. The sequence can be described both with reference to second-formant frequency and to closeness of formants. Cooper and Ross offer no explanation for this finding; but in light of Halle's suggestion, one could extrapolate here the localistic principle they offer for other freezes, "*up* comes before *down*." In what follows, I wish to elaborate the implications of these findings in light of the explanations offered in this work. The plausibility of these explanations increases in view of other parts of Cooper and Ross's article. These authors adduce a whole group of phonological constraints on conjunct ordering. They provide the following rule that governs the constraints (by "place 2 elements," they mean the kind of elements that typically come last in conjuncts):

compared to place 1 elements, place 2 elements contain, other factors being equal:

(a) more syllables
(b) longer resonant nuclei
(c) more initial consonants
(d) a more obstruent initial segment, if both place 1 and place 2 elements start with only one consonant
(e) vowel containing a lower second formant frequency
(f) fewer final consonants
(g) a less obstruent final segment, if both place 1 and place 2 elements end in a single consonant. (ibid., 71)

In chapter 1, I discussed some instances of (a) and (e). An instance of (b) would be "Trick or treat"; of (c) would be "by hook or by crook"; of (d)—"walkie-talkie"; of (f)—"betwixt and between"; of (g)—"hit or miss." For the sake of (d) and (g), the authors represent the gradient of obstruency to which they adhere in the following (decreasing) order:

T[stops]—S[spirants]—N[nasals]—L[liquids]—G[glides].

Phonetically, this represents a decreasing order of effort required to overcome articulatory obstructions. In view of our discussions of the features [±CONTINUOUS] and [±PERIODIC], a decreasing perceptual effort also may be indicated.

It should be noticed that our description of (e) not only suggests an explanation for the examples accounted for by it, but also that this explanation is *of the same kind* as the ones that can be offered for the other constraints in the list: (a), (b), and (c) can be described by the rule "the longer member comes last." According to the present view, (d) and (e) can be described as "the member that exerts greater processing effort comes last." Items (f) and (g), however, appear to pose a problem. Here, the member that exerts the smaller effort comes last.

Taken together, (c), (d), (f), and (g) suggest that in the respect considered here, consonants and consonant clusters function differently at the beginning and at the end of words. This is precisely one of the main implications of the present section. We have found that speech sounds may be used as "arbitrary linguistic signs," combined into words by a syntagmatic relationship, forming entities of linguistic value; at the same time, there may be a nonreferential combination of the same sounds, based on repetition. We have also discovered in Roger Brown's TOT experiment that the cognitive system seems to handle speech sounds differently in these two kinds of sound pattern, accuracy being *relatively* better at the beginning for ss words and relatively better at the end for sm words. Now consider the following minimal pairs listed by Cooper and Ross as examples of (g): "kith or kin," "push and pull," "spic and span," "might and main," "rock and roll," "thick and thin." For these minimal pairs at least, it will be fair to assume that the importance of their sound patterns overrides the semantic ingredient. Thus, as might be expected from Brown's findings, and in the context of phonological constraints on word order, we might suggest that in these minimal pairs the attenuation of the final consonant or consonant cluster in the last member of the conjunction increases the *relative* weight of the consonant or consonant cluster at its beginning.[6]

6. I am indebted to Ronith Shoshoni, who brought to my attention the article by Cooper and Ross.

To Sum Up

This chapter has been devoted to the relationship between musicality in verse and Jakobson's model of child phonology and phonological universals. Two aspects of this model were found to be relevant to our aesthetic interest: an initial distinction between the referential and nonreferential (babbling) use of speech sounds by the infant; and the *order* of acquisition of speech sounds for referential use. The nonreferential use is emotionally charged and the referential use is typically correlated with rational and volitional control. Poetic language typically superimposes the former use on the latter, affording pleasure derived from regression to an earlier mode of cognitive functioning in a publicly respectable manner. As for the order of acquisition, I have suggested that the later the acquisition of a certain speech sound for arbitrary linguistic use, the more it amplifies those poetic effects (discussed at length in chapter 1) that arise from such characteristics of speech sounds as their relative encodedness, continuity, and periodicity. Nasal vowels are among the child's latest acquisitions (and correspondingly rare in the world's languages); they are periodical, and relatively much precategorical sensory information reaches awareness by way of their perception. The perceptual and emotional qualities typically associated with these characteristics are amplified in these late acquisitions to an extreme degree, generating unusually intense poetic potentials. That seems to be an important reason for their relative abundance and prominence in Symbolist poetry. Accordingly, the greater part of this chapter has been devoted to examining how nasal vowels are exploited in nineteenth- and twentieth-century French and Hungarian Symbolist poetry.

It has been suggested that the emotional difference between the referential and nonreferential use of speech sounds may correspond to a difference in cognitive processing: the former tends to focus attention on the final positions of words, whereas the latter focuses on the initial positions. It has been pointed out that since syllable final formants have been observed to have transitions of greater duration and greater frequency change than have initial transitions, final consonants offer a greater amount of sensory information and may be easier to perceive. These observations may account for an intuitively felt (and statistically established) difference between Milton's and Spenser's use of consonant clusters. In a coda we have revisited an issue discussed in chapter 1. In a sequence of two or more coordinate items, it is most natural for the one that requires the greatest processing effort to come last. Cooper and Ross have extensively examined word order in "frozen conjuncts" and formulated a wide range of semantic and phonological constraints on word order in such phrases. I have suggested that the processing difference between syllable final and initial consonant clusters discussed in the preceding section may help us establish a set of homogeneous rules governing the phonological constraints established by Cooper and Ross.

Tactile Metaphors for Sounds

Setting the Problem

The essay that constitutes chapter 1 has been criticized as follows:

> The paper discusses, among other things, the shared intuition that
> the transition from /u/ to /i/ is more like an upward step than
> like a downward step, and attempts to account for this intuition by
> pointing to the fact that the second formant of /i/ (2,900 cps) is
> higher than the second formant of /u/ (700 cps). This is a simple
> and beautiful explanation *if* we know why the frequency of 2,900
> cps is called "higher" than the frequency of 700. Without an ex-
> planation why do we use the same adjective—"high"—to describe
> a skyscraper as well as a soprano voice, we merely transfer the
> mystery from one place to another.

I could defend my position by saying that every inquiry must be cut off
at some arbitrary point. Suffice it for my purpose in cognitive poetics
that there is considerable intersubjective and intercultural agreement
that the transition from bass sounds to treble sounds is more like an
upward than a downward step. In other words, granting the point of
the criticism, the account in question may still have explanatory power,
since it explains why an /i/ and an /u/ uttered at the *same fundamental
pitch* are felt to differ, *somehow*, in pitch, and why this felt difference
corresponds to certain known differences between sound frequencies.
An inquiry into the shared intuition concerning the spatial qualities
attributed to frequency differences between sounds would take me far

beyond the scope of cognitive poetics. I have decided, nevertheless, to take up the challenge and add a more general essay, mainly for two reasons: first, because the inquiry promised intriguing results from the very beginning; second, because I found the answers to the questions concerning spatial metaphors for sounds and related issues illuminating and inspiring for cognitive poetics as well. More specifically, the answers suggested below may explain, quite consistently, a considerable number of synaesthetic metaphors that abound in language and literature.

Let me say that one should not hope to find, eventually, some final cause from which all relevant analogies can be derived. But one may hope to find an interrelated system of significant and consistent analogies that appear to make ample sense in view of the available information about the cognitive organization of Man.

Cognitive Organization or Mediated Association?

To meet the above criticism, I am going to consider several aspects of the spatial metaphor for sounds. I shall embrace two of the prevalent assumptions in this matter, one being that spatial organization is of central importance in human cognition, the other that when the learner of the language learns the general spatial model, he can productively derive many further expressions applying spatial words to nonspatial notions such as sound qualities or emotional states.

Sounds can be located along dimensions whose extremes are marked by spatial notions such as LOW~HIGH, THICK~THIN, or space-related notions such as HEAVY~LIGHT. These dimensions seem to be correlated in certain meaningful ways. There is plenty of anecdotal as well as carefully controlled experimental evidence to indicate that intuitions concerning the spatial as well as the tactile qualities of sound are fairly consistent from observer to observer, and even from culture to culture. Such experiments have been reported by Roger Brown in his classic of psycholinguistics (1968: 110–54). That whole chapter testifies to Brown's usually brilliant insights and subtle ways of analysis. Here, however, I am going to quote only two passages with which I disagree.

> A concept like "boulder" is referred to rocks and stone and, in comparison, judged to be "heavy," "large," "thick," and "wide." These terms are directly applicable to boulders. However, boulders have no voices. Where, then, does the concept belong on the

"bass-treble" or "loud-soft" scales? We cannot doubt the answer. If Disney were to give a boulder a voice it would be "bass" and "loud" in contrast to the piping of a pebble. This could be a mediated association: a boulder must have a bass voice because creatures that do have bass voices are usually heavy and boulders are heavy. It is not necessary to assume that there is any subtle inter-sensory quality found in boulders and bass voices.

Subjects in the study of Brown et al. felt that "thick" and "thin" simply do not apply to voices. However, "loud" and "resonant" do. Now thick people and animals and violin strings are usually loud and resonant. So, if the subject is required to guess, he will call the loud and resonant voice "thick." This need not be because the voice shares some inter-sensory quality with the visual or tactile apprehension of thickness. It could be because the voice is loud and creatures who have loud voices are usually thick, a mediated association. (152–53)

Brown himself seems to be less than happy with such an explanation, and rather than mediative associations, he seems to prefer more direct associations—the kind of explanation he offers to phrases such as "cold manners" and "cold voices." "Perhaps, whenever people behave in an unfriendly fashion their skin temperatures fall below the level of people who behave in a friendly fashion. We should have to assume this to be true whatever form unfriendliness may assume in a given culture" (149).

The cognitive approach to Man, of which Brown is one of the most outstanding exponents, tends to regard explanations such as mediated associations as the last resort of the scientist, where all structural explanations fail. What seems to be wrong with the mediated associations theory is that it reverts to a rather strong version of associationist theory, assuming that people in various cultures have been uniformly conditioned by external conditions. It is all too easy to invent some mediating story that appears to be pretty convincing, until one becomes aware of not less convincing counterexamples.[1] Thus, the color red

1. One could perhaps make a good case for a structuralist version of the mediated associations theory. For instance, the BOULDER~PEBBLE opposition is perceived as analogous to the ADULT~CHILD opposition by virtue of their relationship to the BIG~SMALL opposition. According to Rosch and Mervis's "best example" theory, the greatest contrast between adult and child in the voice dimension will be manifest in the BASS~TREBLE opposition. Such an analogy may *reinforce* the intersense analogy expounded below,

is felt to be warm, whereas blue is felt to be cold; this feeling is not culture-dependent and thus cannot be explained by cultural conditioning. There is a rather widely accepted explanation that fire is red in all cultures, while the blue sea is considered relatively cold. However, the blue sky on a tropical (or even European) summer noon is not associated with cold. The sun at its hottest would be associated with gold rather than red, whereas red would be associated with the setting sun rather than the shining sun.[2]

Space-Sound Analogy: A Structural Account

I submit that bass voices are perceived as thicker than soprano voices, not because creatures that do have bass voices are usually thick and heavy, but precisely because "they share some inter-sensory quality with the visual or tactile apprehension of thickness." (I happen to know quite a few thick and heavy opera singers who have tenor or even coloratura voices.) Whereas the relationship between thick people and bass voices appears to be quite incidental, the relationship between thick violin strings and thick and low sounds seems to have good physical causes. Sounds are vibrations of the air or some other material medium. The thicker the string, *other things being equal*, the *slower* and

---

which I consider as the primary justification for the identification of thickness with bass voices.

2. Such associationist explanations appear particularly naive when one coniders some possible physiological-structural explanations:

> Féré found that muscular power and blood circulation are increased by colored light "in the sequence from blue—least, through green, yellow, orange, red." This agrees well with the psychological observations on the effect of these colors, but there is no telling whether we are dealing here with a secondary consequence of the perceptual phenomenon or whether there is a more direct nervous influence of light energy on motor behavior and blood circulation. (Arnheim, 1967: 327)

Further, Arnheim describes Goldstein's investigation of certain mental phenomena in patients with a certain brain defect.

> When the patient looked at a yellow paper his arm, controlled by the defective brain center, would deviate about 55 centimeters from the midline, the deviation was 50 centimeters for red, 45 centimeters for white, 42 centimeters for blue, 40 centimeters for green. When he closed his eyes the deviation was 70 centimeters. Goldstein concluded that the colors corresponding to long wavelengths go with an expansive reaction, whereas the short lengths make for constriction. . . . This physical reaction is paralleled by the painter Kandinsky's remarks on the appearance of colors. (ibid.)

wider the vibrations. (Not so with singers: when they get fatter or thinner, their voice range and voice quality remain essentially unchanged.)

There are, then, at least three physical dimensions that are analogous and covarying: SLOW~FAST, WIDE~NARROW, and THICK~THIN. The first two pairs of adjectives describe the vibrations, the third pair describes the strings (if there be any) that may be causally related to the first two. It should be noted, however, that whereas the THICK~THIN pair characterizes the source of the sound and may be extended to the distal stimulus (the perceived sound), only by way of some conditioned reflex do the SLOW~FAST and the WIDE~NARROW pairs characterize the proximal stimulus that actually hits the membrane of the ear and is directly experienced. In chapter 1, I have quoted Polányi saying that the qualities of the "proximal term of tacit knowledge" (and, one might add, of perception) are typically displaced away from us to the distal term. Phenomenologically, the relative frequency and width of sound vibrations are experienced as their relative height and thickness, respectively.

Localism

To understand the nature of correspondences of the scale of frequency with the scale of height, we must adopt a localistic view of language and of cognitive functioning. In this discussion I shall rely on Miller and Johnson-Laird (1976: 375–410), Clark and Clark (1977: 426–28, 538–39), Lyons (1977: 690–703; 718–24), and Shepard (1981). "The term *localism* is being used here to refer to the hypothesis that spatial expressions are more basic, grammatically and semantically, than various kinds of non-spatial expressions . . . , they serve as structural templates, as it were, for other expressions; and the reason why this should be so, it is plausibly suggested by psychologists, is that spatial organization is of central importance in human cognition" (Lyons, 1977: 718). Some psychologists (for example, Roger Shepard) believe that cognitive mechanisms responsible for linguistic transformations are derived from cognitive mechanisms that were originally evolved for spatial transformations.

At any rate, the succession of sounds gradually changing in their frequency are perceived within the spatial template of a ladder or scale. The word *pitch*, for instance, means, according to the *American College Dictionary*, "a point, position, or degree, as in a scale"; whereas *scale* means "a succession or progression of steps or degrees; a graduated series." A musical scale is literally such a "graduated series;" the succession of sounds is arranged in the order of their gradually changing frequencies. It is precisely these similar structures that enable (or compel) us to think of the succession of sounds in terms of a spatial scale. Why should this scale be placed in an upward rather than in a left-to-right or in a back-to-front position? After all, keyboard instruments would suggest a left-to-right position, whereas the violin would suggest front-to-back; what is more, the cello would suggest an upside-down position. Past experience with the most familiar musical instruments can hardly account for the upward position of the scale. Some generalizations of the localists, however, can easily account for it.

> Directionality in the vertical dimension—i.e. the difference between upwards and downwards—is established by our experience of the effects of the force of gravity, by the fact that, normally, the sky is above us and the ground beneath us and by the asymmetry of the human body in the vertical dimension. For these, and other reasons, verticality is physically and psychologically the most salient of the spatial dimensions.
>
> There are two horizontal dimensions, neither of which is fixed, in the way that verticality is, by the force of gravity or anything comparable. . . . But [man] is asymmetrical in one of the two horizontal dimensions, and symmetrical in the other: i.e. he has a front and a back, and two symmetrical sides. He has his principal organs of speech directed towards the region in front of him. . . . The asymmetrical front-back dimension is less salient than the vertical direction, but more salient than the symmetrical right-left dimension. (Lyons, 1977: 690–91)

This account is far from being ad hoc. It is a fairly principled description of what appears to be "just those dimensions the human perceptual apparatus is tuned to pick out," as the Clarks succinctly put it (Clark and Clark, 1977: 534).

Marked and Unmarked Adjectives

These dimensions, thus described, may explain a large number of cognitive and linguistic phenomena, among them the intriguing marked and unmarked adjectives. They serve as the basis of a long series of most significant distinctions. On the basis of Lyons's description, we should predict that a scale of sounds would be perceived in a vertical rather than a horizontal direction. Should the vertical direction be barred for some reason, we should predict that spatial relations between percepts or ideas would be in a front-back direction, as, for example, "backward" political views or educational methods. Such notions as "left-wing" or "right-wing" policies are intuitively judged as more arbitrary, more convention-dependent, than "backward" policies. This can be confirmed by a thought-experiment that could easily be translated into a real experiment. Imagine asking people whether we could rename by convention (a) communist policies as "right-wing" and fascist policies as "left-wing" (or even a "right" deed as "sinister" or vice versa); (b) outdated policies as "advanced" and policies based on recent social theories as "backward"; (c) slow vibrations as "high" sounds and fast vibrations as "low" sounds. Then imagine asking them to grade these renamings according to their intuitive acceptability. There appears to be a good chance that (a) would be the most acceptable of the three, and (c) the least acceptable. It should be noted concerning (a) that "right-wing" and "left-wing" policies would be regarded as rather arbitrary conventions, whereas "right" and "sinister" in their capacity of referring to spatial directions as well as to moral judgments would be felt to be dead metaphors or etymologically related (or even incidental) homonyms, ultimately related to some arbitrary convention. "Advanced" and "backward" policies, or "high" and "low" tones, on the contrary, would be felt to be just the right metaphors.

In describing the succession of sounds, I have used such pairs of antonyms as HIGH~LOW, FAST~SLOW, THICK~THIN, WIDE~NARROW. The terms of each pair designate the extremes of one scale and may be defined as the polar opposite of the other; they can be graded in each other's terms. That which is slower is less fast, and that which is faster is less slow; that which is thinner is less thick, and that which is thicker is less thin; and so forth. Notwithstanding, the two terms of a pair are far from being symmetrical. One term of each pair is relatively unmarked. One may ask, "how long is the movie?" But not "how short is the movie?" when one does not know whether the movie was long or short for a movie. Likewise, one may say "two hours' long," but not "two hours' short" (see Clark and Clark, 1977: 427). "Long" in this case is the unmarked term of the pair that may designate both the whole scale and one of its extremes.

If we can account for the asymmetry of these pairs of opposite terms, we might also explain why the high extreme of the height scale corre-

sponds to the fast (high frequency) extreme of the frequency scale, and
the low extreme to the slow (low frequency) extreme, rather than the
other way around.

> In English, dimensions are described with adjectives like *high* and
> *low*, *wide* and *narrow*, *far* and *near*, and *thick* and *thin*. In each pair
> the first adjective describes lack of extent. But there is an extraor-
> dinary consistency among these adjectives. The terms that describe
> "having extent" are all linguistically unmarked and positive; the
> terms that describe "lacking extent" are linguistically marked and
> negative. What is even more remarkable is that . . . this is true
> in all languages. . . . Moreover, children seem to attend more to
> the objects that "have extent" than to those that "lack extent" and
> this appears to explain why they typically learn the words for the
> positive ends of such dimensions first. (Clark and Clark, 1977: 533)

Intersensory Analogies

The terms that denote having more or consisting of more are, then,
unmarked and positive, whereas the terms that denote having less are
marked and negative. The rule is that *the unmarked ends of the analogous
scales correspond to each other*. Thus, fast vibrations are perceived as high
tones, slow vibrations as low tones.[3]

So, if we experience sounds as low or high, thick or thin, we need
not have recourse to mediated associations as an explanation. Good
perceptual reasons, deeply rooted in the organization of the human
perceptual apparatus, account for this phenomenon. If we realize that
sounds of various pitches differ in the width of their vibration (or
wavelength), we may quite safely assume that bass voices do share
"some intersensory quality with the visual or tactile apprehension of
thickness." The relationship between the "height" and the frequency

---

3. What is the point of reference for high or low? "Ground level is used in judging
something as high or low, unless some other plane of reference supersedes it. It is normally taken to be zero height" (Clark and Clark, 1977: 534). Self's height is perceived as
roughly corresponding to the mid-range of sounds, low sounds as lower than self, high
sounds as higher than self. We have characterized sounds as vibrations of certain rates
of recurrence (frequencies); frequency is negatively correlated with wavelength. Notice
that the HIGH-LOW dimension serves as a spatial template for the nonspatial scale of frequencies, and *not* for the spatial dimension of wavelength; that is, the unmarked term
high is felt to correspond to the unmarked term *great* (indeed, *high*) frequency and not to
the unmarked term "*long* wave."

of sounds is somewhat more complex. If we accept—as I believe we should—the localist assumption that spatial expressions serve as templates for nonspatial expressions because spatial organization is of central importance in human cognition, we ought to predict for good (though rather complex) perceptual reasons that treble voices will be felt to be higher than bass voices. *Greater height and more frequent vibrations are the unmarked (more salient) extremes of their respective scales, and thus they are matched.*

As for the THICK~THIN characterization of sounds, an additional observation seems to be pertinent. The sounds we usually hear do not consist of fundamentals only, but of overtones. Since the range of frequencies audible to the human ear is limited, and since there are no undertones, the lower the fundamental, the greater the number of overtones within the human ear's range. Thus, when we strike a key near the left end of the piano keyboard, we perceive a thick aura of overtones around the sound that is absent from the sounds produced by striking the keys near the right end. (Notice, by the way, that in spite of the left-to-right arrangement of the keyboard, we perceive the piano sounds as low or high rather than left-wing or right-wing as it would be predicted by a mediated association theory.)

Trouble with the Foregoing Conception

At this point our discussion seems to run into serious trouble. Sounds of *greater* frequencies also have, necessarily, *smaller* wavelength; sounds of *smaller* frequencies have *greater* wavelength. Accordingly, lower sounds are perceived as thicker and heavier than higher ones. Small frequency is a marked property of sounds, whereas thick and heavy are unmarked qualities on their respective scales. Why do we perceive greater frequency rather than thickness or heaviness as analogous to high (as opposed to low)? There appear to be very good linguistic reasons to believe that in many cultures, high-frequency speech sounds are used to characterize small or near objects, low-frequency sounds to characterize large or distant objects. By examining a total of 136 languages, Ultan (1978) tested the hypothesis that diminutive sound symbolism is associated with marked phonological features (high and/or front vowels and palatal or fronted consonants). This, of course, would confirm our assumption that *small* is marked, but disconfirm our assumption that *high* frequency is unmarked. Ultan found that diminutive is most often symbolized by high or high front vowels, high tone, or various kinds of consonantal ablaut. Proximal distance is symbolized overwhelmingly by front or high vowels. To take a language not included in his sample, my native Hungarian, *itt* means "here," *ott* means "there," *ez* means "this," *az* means "that." *Így* means "in this fashion," *úgy* means "in that fashion"; *ide* means "to this place," *oda* "to that place"; *ekkor* "at this time," *akkor* "at that time"; *ekkora* "of this size," *akkora* "of that size," and so forth.[4] "Since high front vowels reflect proportionately higher second formant frequencies, and the higher the tone the higher the natural frequency, there appears a correspondence between a feature of high frequency (= short wavelength in physical terms) and the category of small size" (Ultan, 1978: 545).

Primary and Secondary Analogies

All of this appears to cause trouble for the present conception only as long as we conceive of the interrelation of perceptual spaces as a single kind of interrelation. Michael Kubovy, however, puts forward two hypotheses concerning the interrelation of perceptual spaces. "I have called the first hypothesis the *unified space hypothesis* and the second the *analogous space hypothesis*. According to the first hypothesis a mental representation of space is constructed, so as to integrate our sensory-motor interaction with objects in space. According to the second hypothesis, each sense is sui generis, but interesting analogies hold between some of the dimensions of different senses."

I submit, first, that both hypotheses apply to our field of inquiry, and second, that there is a hierarchic order of their application. Accordingly, sounds are unified entities that, physically, have a temporal dimension (frequency) and a spatial dimension (wavelength). Phenomenologically, these dimensions are experienced as pitch and thickness. As we have noted, marked frequencies *entail* unmarked wavelengths, and unmarked frequencies *entail* marked wavelengths. It is impossible to match the marked end of one dimension with the marked end of the other because the unmatched poles characterize different dimensions of the same entity. At a higher level the temporal scale of sound frequencies is perceived as analogous to the spatial scale of height. I claim that this analogy is dominant, prior to the one discussed

4. It should be noted, nevertheless, that some of these Hungarian pairs seem to be derivatives of such basic pairs as *itt-ott*, *ez-az*.

by Ultan relating high sounds to small objects or proximal distances. We may regard the analogies discussed by Ultan as secondary.

Admittedly, frequency and wavelength are interdependent attributes of sound; when one changes, the other changes too in a predictable direction and measure. Why should we grant the former precedence over the latter? This is because, according to Kubovy (1981), frequency is an indispensable attribute of sound, whereas wavelength is not. *Indispensable* is used here in a technical sense, the criterion for which is not the possibility of existence, but what Kubovy calls "perceptual numerosity." Kubovy introduces these notions by way of a thought-experiment.

> In the experiment, the observer is shown a discrete stimulus and is asked to say how many "entities" are visible in the stimulus, i.e., to judge its *perceptual numerosity*. For instance the stimulus described above, consisting of two well-separated patches of color, one red and the other green, will most likely elicit a *perceptual numerosity* judgment of "two." . . . If, on the other hand, we had transformed the stimulus in the spatial domain so that the two patches were indistinguishable spatially [that is, if we had projected for instance the color patches upon the same location], we would expect an observer to report just one entity. In visual stimuli which vary along the two dimensions of wavelength and spatial location, variation in spatial location is necessary for these stimuli to be perceived as consisting of multiple entities. Roughly, this is what we mean when we refer to indispensable attributes: without variation on these dimensions, accurate report of numerosity is not possible.

This is why for visual perception, spatial location is an "indispensable attribute," whereas wavelength is not. As for the time dimension of sounds, Kubovy distinguishes *micro-time* and *event-time*. The former covers pitch-generating periods, the interaural time differences. "When events are separated by such small time intervals, they will be perceived to be fused, and not successive. Event time covers the range of times between acoustic events that are perceived as distinct, successive events."

To show that the time dimension is the indispensable attribute of aural perception, Kubovy offers another thought-experiment. Imagine two loudspeakers, one to the right, one to the left of a blindfolded listener.

Suppose the lefthand speaker emitted an A4 (440 Hz) and the right-hand speaker emitted an E5 (659.3 Hz). The listener would report hearing two tones. If both tones were played over the left-hand speaker, while the right-hand speaker were silent, the listener would still report hearing two tones. If, however, both speakers emitted an A4, the listener would report hearing only one tone, originating from a point in space between the two loud-speakers. Therefore an auditory stimulus cannot be perceptually numerous if it is distributed over space alone, i.e., without being distributed over frequency (and/or event time). Thus, frequency and event time are indispensable attributes of audition, whereas spatial location is not.

It should be noted parenthetically that when we listen to stereo music through two loudspeakers (or, for that matter, a pair of earphones) and are able to locate the various instruments in space between the two speakers, the system uses the fact that people can localize sounds primarily on the basis of time and intensity differences at the two ears.

Kubovy does not show, as he did with respect to visual perception, that wavelength is not an indispensable attribute of audition (actually, he could argue by the same token that frequency is not an indispens-able attribute of vision, since wavelength and frequency are negatively correlated in the physical aspect of color in the same way as in the physi-cal aspect of sound). The only reason (and quite a good one) for us to assume that frequency rather than wavelength is the indispensable attribute of audition is that it is more parsimonious to account for both ways of achieving numerosity with the help of one dimension than with two, that is, the *time dimension* (micro-time and event-time) than with wavelength and event-time.

The Ontogenesis of an Intersensory Analogy

It should be pretty clear by now that the analogy between sound fre-quency and spatial vertical dimension is basic in human cognition. It is certain, at any rate, that we have little conscious control over this analogy and cannot invert at will the matching of its extremes or sus-pend it altogether. So, if it is not transmitted in the structure of the human brain, we ought to look for its origin at a very early stage of the emergence of the individual's consciousness. In an attempt to account for this, I shall follow some of Neisser's arguments (1976) concerning sound perception. First, let us note a certain analogy between seeing and hearing, with a twist of asymmetry in it: "The English language is misleading in this respect: it allows us to say that we hear *sounds* when we are really hearing events, but makes it unreasonable to say that we see *light* when we are really seeing objects. Actually, the two cases are really analogous. We see events (or objects) by means of the information available in light, and hear them by means of the information available in sound" (Neisser, 1976: 158).

I do not think English or any other language is to blame for this asymmetry, but rather the cause is an underlying cognitive difference between the two sensory modes. Neisser implicitly admits this difference: "Sounds inform us about events. While vision and touch enable us to explore stationary environments, hearing tells us only about movement and change" (155). In other words, the light that strikes the retina is a *sign* of stable, unchanging objects, whereas the sound that strikes our ear membrane is a *sign* of such transient entities as movement and change with fairly reliable information about the direction in which they take place, but only vague information about the moving, changing object itself, such as its relative volume, relative hardness, etc. Since light gives us information about comfortably stable objects, we may shift our attention from the sign to the object signified and explore its properties at leisure. Information about ever-changing events is given to us by sound, so we have to delay our attention as long as possible at the sign to be able to detect any further change. Sound thus described is similar in an important respect to such mechanisms of *fast orientation* called "attitudes" or "affects" which I have described elsewhere (Tsur, 1983a: 22; also Tsur, 1992, chapter 1) as having in one's processing space a considerable amount of precategorical (or lowly categorized) information. We seem to handle relatively large lumps of such information, make relatively crude but *quick* judgments about them, and extract no precise information. It gives the organism great flexibility, an adaptability to ever-changing environments. Sound gives less reliable information about the direction and size of an object than vision, less reliable information about the relative hardness of its material, and no information at all about its shape. But the information it does give is very quickly available.

It should be parenthetically noted that one of the basic assumptions of cognitive poetics is that in a rapidly changing environment there is a tendency to cling more consistently to signifiers so as to enable constant checking if one's cognitive apparatus is appropriately tuned to reality. At a higher level of consciousness, this assumption can explain important stylistic differences between uses of figurative language and their typical correlation with certain kinds of social backgrounds (Tsur, 1983a: 45–48; 1987: 196–200; 1992, chapter 15).

So while in the visual mode we are inclined to *attend away from* the signifier to the object signified, in the auditory mode we are inclined to *attend to* the ever-changing, labile signifier so as to be able to detect any minute change in our environment. Thus, the former mode is more accurate in supplying information about unchanging properties of stable objects, whereas the latter mode is more flexible in conveying information about minute changes. Being used essentially as a medium for fast orientation, we seem to be more inclined to grant the sound-signifier much greater flexibility than the light signifier.

> While people can localize sounds rather accurately when it is important to do so (primarily on the basis of time and intensity differences at the two ears), this localization is labile and easily influenced by other factors. No matter where the loudspeakers in the theater may be located, we generally tend to hear the speech as if it came from the actors portrayed on the screen. . . . Sound has a way of insinuating itself into perceptual cycles where it actually does not belong, of being "referred" to events other than those that actually gave rise to it. This property may be important in the acquisition of language. (Neisser, 1976: 162)

One of Neisser's most brilliant speculations concerns the attribution of concrete referents to words. Words specify their referents as well as the speaker's articulatory gestures. Sounds, as we have seen, specify events; speech sounds specify articulatory events (otherwise we could not perceive phonemes in the way we perceive them; see chapter 1). On the other hand, sounds are easily shifted to perceptible motions where they do not actually belong. Imagine a child attending to some object or event. Suppose, the dog walks into the room, and his mother says "Doggie."

> The lucky child is engaged in two perceptual cycles at once. He is picking up information about his mother (she is speaking) and about the dog (it has just come into the room). He is, we may assume, temporarily more interested in the dog. The new information is acoustic, which means that it can be rather freely appropri-

ated by any ongoing perceptual cycle. What is more natural than that he comes to treat it as some sort of attribute of the dog? (165)

It should be noted that children at a very early age are alert to this flexibility of sounds. Neisser mentions empirical evidence provided by Spelke, who presented two movies on adjacent screens to three-month-old babies and played the sound track corresponding to one of the films through a centrally located loudspeaker. The babies looked mostly at the film that corresponded to the auditory information (ibid., 68).

Until now we have considered one kind of evidence of the flexibility of sounds, namely, that auditory patterns are attracted to visual events. A further step is required to explain how sound frequencies became associated with the stationary vertical dimension. There is some evidence that not only movement but also visual salience attracts sound. "Several experiments have shown that the perceived directions of sound sources in a dark room are attracted toward visible points of light" (174–75). Since the vertical is the most salient of spatial dimensions, we might reasonably speculate that infants prior to, or around, the age of three months, when their spatial orientation as well as sensory modes are still lowly differentiated, come to associate the scale of sound frequencies with the scale of vertical dimension.

Recoding Auditory Information

We have considered at some length the nature of the analogy between frequency and spatial vertical direction. We might now further venture and ask, why do we need this analogy? It is one thing to explain the fact that it is vertical rather than horizontal dimension that is analogous to sound frequency. Or it is frequency rather than wavelength that is to be treated as analogous to vertical dimension? And it is another thing to explain the very need for such an analogy.

It seems to me that this analogy handles noncategorical sensory information. As we have seen, sound is a lowly differentiated, rapidly changing stream of information, consisting of minute stimuli that most accurately signal change. We can discriminate such rich sensory sound information only as long as it reverberates in echoic memory, that is, for a few seconds only. To store auditory information for longer periods, it must be recoded in some more stable form less dependent on the niceties of unique sensory information and more easily managed by memory. For present purposes, there appear to be two such ways of recoding: categorization into a phonetic code, and translation into a code of spatial relationships (of a more stable nature).

The first of these codes uses a system of abstract linguistic categories that lend themselves to relatively lengthy storage, but at the price of excluding most of the acoustic information. The second code exploits the fact that spatial organization is of a more stable nature than the sequence of sounds, and that it is of central importance in human cognition: it conceives of the relation between sounds as spatial. Thus, if we cannot remember the exact sensory information about a sound, we still can recall the exact relationship between several sounds, that is, a scale or melody. The spatial structural template not only enables us to remember relations between sounds, but it also enables us to better differentiate between them. The role of the spatial structural template in differentiating sound frequencies will be more readily apparent if we compare this sound dimension to some other dimension, say, loudness, where no such spatial analogue is readily available. On this dimension we can easily differentiate the extremes and perhaps a few intermediate degrees of loudness. Now, suppose one hears a single tone of unchanging frequency with changing degrees of loudness. How many degrees of loudness will one be able to discriminate? And for how long will the sequence of those degrees of loudness be remembered? Should we wonder, then, that works of music are primarily composed of sounds of changing frequencies rather than changing amplitudes?

These two ways of recoding are readily illustrated by the experiments that introduced the issue of categorical perception in chapter 1. The syllables /ba, da, ga/ differ from one another only in the onset frequency of their second formant transitions. If one divides the frequency range between /ba/ and /ga/ into, say, fourteen equal steps, and plays back only the series of excised second formant transitions, one receives a *rising series* of glides (spatial relationship). If, however, one plays back the series of fourteen unmutilated sound patterns, one receives a series of /ba, da, ga/ syllables; *no rising series* of sound patterns will be detected. The change from one category to another will not be gradual, but abrupt; discrimination between two successive steps will be quite good across category boundaries, but poor within categories. Here, the unique sensory information is rather poorly discriminated, and even more poorly remembered (even for a few seconds). But if asked, "What did the man say an hour (or a week, or a month) ago?," one may quite accurately answer, "The man said 'ba.'"

Suppose we tried to train a student of phonetics to tell whether some isolated formant transition cued a /ba/ or a /da/; this might prove well nigh impossible. Our performance is quite poor in the absolute judgment of auditory sense information that is neither linguistically categorized nor perceived as part of a (spatial) structural template. It will be much easier to train a student to discriminate an isolated formant transition cuing a /ba/ from one cuing a /ga/, since the former is likely to be an *upward* glide, whereas the latter will be *downward*.

Differentiation

When the human ear picks up a sound of a certain frequency, the sound's several hundreds or thousands of vibrations per second exceeds the ear's capacity to resolve them; it fuses them into a unitary event categorized as a sound of a certain pitch. Sounds of various pitches are easily differentiated, pitch (frequency) being an indispensable attribute of auditory perception. As we have seen, the most highly differentiated dimension of sound, frequency, is perceived within a structural template of the most highly differentiated dimension of spatial orientation. This spatial template increases the differentiation of the sound continuum.

However, the sensory information of sounds has some less differentiated aspects. First and foremost, we should mention a highly divergated overtone structure. This overtone structure, too, exceeds by far the human ear's resolving power. So its components are fused into a unique and unitary quality, usually called tone color. In Polányi's terms, one might say that we attend away from overtone structure to tone color; the latter is the meaning of the former. Tone color differs from one overtone structure to another; tone colors are fairly discriminable, although they have no category names comparable to visual colors. We usually label tone colors by the name of their characteristic sources, for example, wooden or metallic sound. It should not be very surprising that for visual colors we have stable category names, whereas we call sound colors by the name of their sources. We usually see stable objects with stable properties (and, as Neisser noted, not light). But we hear the sound *of* objects in change or in motion. An experienced listener can make quite fine distinctions; within metallic color, for instance, he may discriminate the sound of a trumpet from that of a French horn.

On a specific level, tone colors have little in common with visual color, and it would be odd to talk about green or mauve sounds. Even when

Oscar Wilde does use such phrases, they are regarded as the extrava-
gances of a highly idiosyncratic author. At a higher level of abstraction,
however, the two kinds of color have certain properties in common.
Both are gestalt-free qualities, secondary to the shapes carried by the
indispensable attributes of their respective sensory modes. Both may
diversify or unify substantial areas created by the shapes carried by the
respective indispensable attributes. Both have, further, such tertiary
qualities as brightness, dullness, darkness, and the like. When we apply
to sounds such visual terms as *color* and *brightness*, we usually refer to
some fairly (but not highly) differentiated qualities whose function is to
unify or diversify sound shapes.

Further, sounds also may have qualities that are usually described
by terms derived from the domain of the tactile sense, such as *acute*,
grave, *heavy*, *piercing*, *sharp*, and the like. For reasons that will become
apparent, I should consider *thick* and *thin* as belonging to the tactile
rather than to the visual domain (for our present purposes at least).
In his work on "Panchronistic Tendencies in Synaesthesia," Ullmann
(1957) discovered an overwhelming tendency in Romantic and post-
Romantic poetry of several languages to perform metaphoric transfer
in a direction from the more lowly differentiated sense to the more
highly differentiated one. Keats's famous line

> And taste the music of this vision pale

would be a highly typical instance of this tendency. Here, *vision pale*
of the visual sense is treated in terms of *music* from the less differentiated auditory sense, which, in turn, is treated in terms of *taste*, which is
still less differentiated. To consider more colloquial, less sophisticated
phrases, we might expect to encounter such expressions as *warm sounds*,
soft sounds, *heavy sounds*, *warm colors*, *soft colors*, and even *heavy colors* more
frequently than *loud temperatures*, *green temperatures*, *loud touch*, *green
touch*, *loud weight*, or *green weight* (Donne's *loud perfume* was condemned
by critics as "the concoction of an experience"). As the examples show,
these tendencies are reflected in colloquial expressions as well.

At some variance with Ullmann's explanation, I have elsewhere
(Tsur, 1987: 209–72; 1992, chapter 9) attempted to account for these
tendencies. Human language is a highly differentiated, highly con-
ceptualized tool. It seems to be impossible, therefore, to talk about
evasive, lowly differentiated, nonconceptual, or noncategorical experiences or streams of information (which appear to be at the very core
of poetry). One way to overcome this limitation is to use synaesthetic

metaphor, especially when the transfer proceeds in the upward direction, that is, when we talk about the more differentiated sense in terms of the less differentiated sense. The visual and auditory domains have extremely rich vocabularies, whereas the other sensory domains are each restricted to a small number of pairs of antonymous adjectives, occasionally with one or two adjectives to mark some intermediate position (for example, *cool* and *warm* between *cold* and *hot*). In spite of this, higher sensory domains borrow terms from the lower sensory domains more frequently than the other way around (thus, synaesthetic metaphor is dominated by the principle seen in the biblical tale of the pauper's sheep). Terms of the lower sensory domains are taken to characterize percepts of higher sensory domains (rather than vice versa) whenever we need to characterize some lowly differentiated perceptual or emotional quality. Apart from its possible semantic content, a term of a lower domain transfers to the visual, auditory or emotional experience the feature [-DIFFERENTIATED].

At this point I wish to make a fleeting reference to an important stylistic corollary of this tendency. Upward transfer appears to be the unmarked use of synaesthetic metaphor. This implies that downward transfer should not be nonexistent, but considerably rarer than unmarked transfers, and should be expected to generate some marked effect, such as wit, or witticism, or mannerism, or modernism. Thus, it should be relatively abundant in certain kinds of literary texts, usually described as witty, modernistic, manneristic, and the like.

Let us return to sounds in extralinguistic reality and the specific semantic contents of synaesthetic metaphors. Such tactile metaphors as *sharp, piercing, thin, thick, heavy* sounds are usually used to refer to some lowly differentiated, evasive, nonconceptual, and continuous (that is, noncategorical) qualities of sounds. Speakers who apply such tactile metaphors to sounds are usually incapable of telling what physical property they are designating with these terms, but they feel them to be just the right term. What is more, they mainly agree with each other about the correct application of these terms.

If we ask what are the physical correlates of these perceptual qualities, we should look for them among what might be called dispensable attributes of the physical signal. Auditory information is mainly carried by its temporal dimension, whether micro-time or event-time. Musical shapes are generated by successive sounds, that is, sounds that follow one another in time and differ from one another in frequency (pitch). Another physical aspect of sounds is wavelength. As we have seen, wavelength has a *fixed* relationship to frequency and carries no independent auditory information; so, we attend away from wavelength to frequency and from frequency to pitch. This, however, does not mean that we do not perceive wavelength *at all*, only that very little of the perception reaches consciousness. Likewise, it is overtone structure that generates tone color. Tone color is of great survival value since it gives us a great deal of information about the nature of its source. The *amount* of audible overtones, on the other hand, is redundant, determined—as we have seen—by the overtone structure and the frequency of the fundamental tone. This, again, does not mean that we do not perceive it, only that we attend away from it to other, more vital aspects of sound information. When we feel a sound or sound sequence to be thick or thin, we probably categorize an indiscriminable mixture of subliminally perceived physical aspects of the sound signal (wavelength and amount of audible overtones) as an overall, lowly differentiated perceptual quality. Thick sounds are of greater wavelength than thin sounds and, by the same token, carry a greater burden of subliminally perceived overtones.

One important aspect of applying such spatio-tactile analogues to sound qualities is that one may use them *productively*. When we perceive certain sounds as heavy, others as sharp or piercing, we appear to do just that. To paraphrase Rumelhart (1979: 89, who discusses thermal metaphors): In all of these cases, it would seem much more economical to say, not that the word has two meanings, but that tactile sensations and sound qualities (or emotional states) are analogous to one another in a certain way. The meanings of the terms *thick* and *thin* presumably do not have to be learned independently; rather, the learning of one clearly reinforces and modifies the use of the other. Surely, the learner of the language just learns the general spatial or tactile model and can productively derive these and other cases of applying tactile and spatial words to such nonspatial qualities as sound qualities or emotional states. *Other things being equal*, the thicker the object, the heavier it is. Again, other things being equal, the thinner an object the sharper it is (see also Brown, 1968: 152).

Such productively generated uses may be reinforced by subliminal (and sometimes even consciously perceived) sensations. We perceive sounds through a highly specialized sense organ, the ear. We receive tactile sensations all over the outer surface of our skin. Whoever has listened to a really good stereo system may have experienced—even consciously—that while he *heard* the low, thick sounds through his ears, he had a pleasurable sensation of pressure all over his body, as if he had been plunged into a thick mass of sound. Correspondingly, when sound energy of short wavelength (and of a small amount of audible overtones) is perceived as pressing against a relatively small area of the ear membrane, the resulting feeling may intuitively be categorized as sharp or piercing.

In discussions of these and related issues it is usually granted that, physically, low frequency sounds are of relatively long waves, etc., but I have been asked, more than once, the following question: "Do you believe that people actually perceive the physical shape, or wavelength, of sound waves?" The answer is "yes" and "no." If you ask me to describe the physical shape of the sound wave, as I actually perceive it, I shall have to answer, "I don't know what you are talking about." Nonetheless, we may have, in Benjamin Lee Whorf's words, "certain dim psychic sensations" (see Jakobson and Waugh, 1979: 192) about them. These dim sensations are very elusive; it is impossible to tell where they come from, yet they are very persistent. Any rational person will tell you that it makes little sense to talk about the perceived spatial width or thickness of a sound, yet it is *somehow* right to describe a low sound as thicker than a high sound, and it would be *somehow* wrong to describe a high sound as thicker or wider than a low sound. Any rational person will tell you that if you utter an /i/ and an /u/ *on the same fundamental pitch*, the /i/ cannot be, by definition, higher than the /u/. Nevertheless, it *is* perceived as *somehow* higher. One is tempted to regard the relative height of these vowels as some kind of cultural convention. Yet, intuitively, it would be hardly imaginable that in some remote culture a reverse convention should prevail. It just sounds right to associate the /i/-end of the /u~i/ opposition with the high-end of the HIGH~LOW opposition, and not the other way around. The only way to account for such dim psychic sensations is to assume that certain aspects of the physical signal *are*, subliminally, perceived, and these aspects sometimes do reach consciousness, *however faintly*. That is why we have only elusive, dim, though persistent intuitions about them. Sound waves exert *pressure* not only on our ear membrane, but on the entire outer surface of our skin. Now, it is of the nature of tactile sensations to be more lowly differentiated than aural sensations; this substantial difference is further augmented by the fact that we are biologically programmed to attend away from tactile aspects of the sound waves to their auditory aspects. Nevertheless, enough of the tactile aspects of the sound waves reaches consciousness to give rise to certain vague intuitions, just enough to render it more acceptable to associate one pole of a tactile scale with one pole of the auditory scale than with its opposite.

These preferences, however slight and evasive, are sufficiently persistent to prompt and direct some kind of natural selection process until these intuitive preferences come to be categorized into hard and fast lexical or grammatical or some other kinds of cultural category. The linguistic universals of sound-size symbolism discussed above may be a case in point. Now, if Ehrenzweig (1965) is right, semiconscious, elusive perceptions, though of great emotive import, may be offensive, and there is a tendency to sharpen and harden them into conventional, clearly perceptible categories. On the other hand, we may expect such conventionalizations to occur when the individual cultural program reaches a point when it is intuitively just right. In this respect, D'Andrade's formulation (1980) is most illuminating: "An important assumption of cognitive anthropology is that in the process of repeated social transmission, cultural programs come to take forms which have a good fit to the natural capacities of the human brain. Thus, when similar cultural forms are found in most societies around the world, there is reason to search for psychological factors which could account for these similarities."

Finally, a basic assumption recurring throughout this chapter has been that spatial organization is of enormous importance in cognitive organization. It should be noted, however, that I have carefully avoided any suggestion that audition is a derivative sense, as claimed by Miller and Johnson-Laird. What I have done is to point out certain characteristics of hearing and the ways in which they are conceived to be analogous to, and in which they interact with, the domains of other senses. Most notably, I have pointed out the advantages of recoding sound information in spatial terms, which, as I have argued, is not the only way of recoding. It is one thing to claim that audition is a derivative sense, and another to claim that the recoding of sound information in spatial terms has certain (very great) advantages that the uncoded information lacks.

There is in the human mind a strong reluctance to face, with full consciousness, the products of poetic genius; and this often takes the form of an attempt
to reduce them to something *other*. . . . This, our natural academic tendency,
is of appalling, and insidious, strength. . . . Such scholarship receives a ready,
if ephemeral, acclamation denied to the more authentic and comprehensive
approach. . . . All would clearly be well were it not for the uncomfortable suspicion that it is too often the very essence of poetry, the liquid fire of its veins,
which we are asked to suppress.—Wilson G. Knight, *The Imperial Theme*

Voyelles
A noir, E blanc, I rouge, U vert, O bleu: voyelles,
Je dirais quelque jour vos naissances latentes:
A, noir corset velu des mouches éclatantes
Qui bombinent autour des puanteurs cruelles,

Golfes d'ombres; E, candeurs des vapeurs et des tentes,
Lances des glaciers fiers, rois blancs, frissons d'ombelles;
I, pourpres, sang craché, rires des lèvres belles
Dans la colère ou les ivresses pénitentes;

U, cycles, vibrements divins des mers virides,
Paix des pâtis semés d'animaux, paix de rides
Que l'alchimie imprime aux grands fronts studieux;

O, suprême Clairon plein des strideurs étranges,

Silences traversés des Mondes et des Anges:
—O l'Oméga, rayon violet de Ses Yeux!

Vowels
A black, E white, I red, U green, O blue: vowels,
I shall tell some day your latent [mysterious] births:
A, black velvety corset of brilliant [exploding] flies
Who bombard [assail] around cruel stenches

Gulfs of shadow; E, candors of vapors and of tents,
Lances of proud glaciers, white kings, shivers of cow-parsley;
I, purples, vomited [spat] blood, laughter of beautiful lips
In anger or penitent intoxications;

U, cycles, divine shudderings of bluish-green seas,
The peace of pastures sown with animals, the peace of wrinkles
Which alchemy prints on broad studious foreheads;

O, supreme Clarion full with strange stridors,
Silences crisscrossed by Worlds and by Angels:
—O the Omega, violet ray from His [Her] Eyes!

This chapter attempts to account for the "mysterious" effect of Rimbaud's "Voyelles" reported by so many readers. Within this general framework, it will also attempt to account for the attribution of specific colors to the various vowels.

As for attempting to account for many readers' experience of having had some mysterious insight by way of reading some poem, one may go about it in two diametrically opposed ways. One may search the poem for symbols derived from alchemy or Cabala; or one may attribute the source of the "mysterious insight" to poetic structure, irrespective of the domain from which the symbols of the poem are derived. The issue at stake is whether certain symbols do have some inherent magic power so that by merely mentioning them one may arouse the mystic experience associated with them, or whether all symbols are more or less equal with respect to their capacity of arousing mystic experiences and it is only when they enter into certain poetic structures that they arouse specific kinds of mystic experiences. From what we know about the nature of poetry, the latter seems more likely. In this respect I wish to distinguish mystic poetry from mystic religious systems. Although the two have their roots in similar cognitive structures, a poem must *earn* its way with a wide reading public that does not necessarily accept in advance its basic tenets, whereas mystic religious systems are usually based on a common consent and a fundamental identification of their initiates with certain assumptions and symbols. One might even go as far as to claim that the touchstone for the value of a mystic religious system is its power to evoke the mystic experience in the converted, whereas the touchstone for the value of, say, George Herbert's or Richard Crashaw's poems is—without committing oneself to the "affective fallacy"—their capability of appealing to skeptical readers.

Now what kind of poetic structure should we expect to underlie mystic poetry? And what kind of cognitive structure should we expect as its basis? As may be inferred from my discussion in chapters 1 and 3, the key to the difference between logical, analytic thinking and global experiencing that may yield, among other things, mystic insight is to be sought between differentiated and compact information processing (characteristic of the left, linguistic hemisphere of the brain) and undifferentiated, diffuse information processing (characteristic of the right hemisphere). From the operational point of view, two of our key terms will be thing-free and gestalt-free qualities, borrowed from Ehrenzweig.

What Bergson calls metaphysical intuition is a gestalt-free vision, capable of superimposed perception. Let us hear his own masterful description of surface and depth vision:

"When I direct my attention inward to contemplate my own self . . . I perceive at first, as a crust solidified at the surface, all the perceptions which come to it from the material world. These perceptions are clear, distinct, juxtaposed or juxtaposable one with another; they tend to group themselves into objects. . . . But if I draw myself in from the periphery toward the center . . . I find an altogether different thing. There is beneath these sharply cut crystals and this frozen surface a continuous flux which is not comparable to any flux I have ever seen. There is a succession of states each of which announces that which follows and contains that which precedes it. In reality no one begins or ends, but all extend into each other."

Bergson recognizes that juxtaposition is essential for surface perception, but not for depth perception. To achieve intuition, he gives a practical recipe; he recommends one to visualize at the same time a diversity of objects in superimposition.

"By choosing images as dissimilar as possible, we shall prevent
any one of them from usurping the place of the intuition it is intended to call up, since it would then be driven away at once by
its rivals. By providing that, in spite of their differences of aspects,
they all require from the mind the same kind of attention . . . we
shall gradually accustom consciousness to a particular and clearly
defined disposition." (Ehrenzweig, 1965: 34–35)

Now, with respect to the mystic experience of poetry, this Bergsonian flux—Ehrenzweig's thing-free vision—has two facets. On the one
hand, there are poetic structures that seem to be capable of evoking
it; in fact, poems reported to yield mystic insight are frequently related to some such structure. On the other hand, such poetic structures
offer few or no clear-cut objects or firm points of reference for a sense
of psychological stability. For that reason, they may arouse anxieties
in many readers. These anxieties may explain why so many readers
of poetry are deprived of what Keats called "Negative Capability,"
the capability of "being in uncertainties, mysteries, doubts, without
any irritable reaching after fact and reason," the ability "to make up
one's mind about nothing—to let the mind be a thoroughfare for all
thoughts" (see Tsur, 1975; 1992, chapter 20).

One reliable way of overcoming such anxieties is to achieve certainty
by doing away with the Bergsonian "flux," Ehrenzweig's "thing-free
vision," Keats's "letting the mind be a thoroughfare for all thoughts."
One effective means for this is to disrupt the smooth continuity of the
flux by isolating symbols allegedly derived from alchemy or Cabala,
and "making up one's mind" by attaching some mystic meaning to
them. Consequently, those interpretations of "Voyelles" based on the
symbols of alchemy and Cabala—most notably Enid Starkie's (1961)
and more recently Richer's (1972)—may be regarded, paradoxically
enough, as defense strategies against the anxieties of mystic insight possibly yielded by the poem. Such interpretations remove from the poem
the disturbing element of the mystic experience, while pretending to
enhance it. The same is true, in general, of ideas such as those vigor-
ously rejected by Plessen (1967) "that for the explication of this text one
must look for a 'key' that will open the gate to some sense hidden behind the manifest meaning of the poem" (287), such as R. Faurisson's
view that "in this hermetic sonnet Rimbaud gives us a *blazon of the female
body*" (ibid., 288). Such "keys" are, manifestly, aids for making up one's

mind about the poem more easily and are firm points in which stable meanings can be anchored among the flux of images.

One important point about Rimbaud's poem, in light of the Bergson-Ehrenzweig conception of "thing-free vision" and "metaphysical insight," is that it is focused on the melting point at which the distinct perceptions that "tend to group themselves into objects" pass into the continuous flux of thing-free perceptions. Even those objects that *are* "juxtaposable" are not juxtaposed so as to constitute "a crust solidified on the surface"; and the bulk of the sonnet consists of thing-free and shape-free qualities. This framework renders Plessen's following suggestion highly significant: "But it is not only at the grammatical level that this isolation works: all the objects enumerated in the poem are detached from their natural context, and thus one sees 'rois blancs' (white kings) in the neighborhood of 'frissons d'ombelles' (shivers of cow-parsley), just as we see 'pâtis semés d'animaux' (pastures sown with animals) in juxtaposition with 'rides' (furrows, wrinkles)" (ibid., 295).

Even in some of these solid objects the focus of attention is shifted to some of their abstract qualities, as in "*frissons* d'ombelles" or "*paix* des rides." Within the same framework I wish to consider Rimbaud's remarkable use of abstract nouns in the plural: "naissances latentes . . . puanteurs cruelles . . . candeurs des vapeurs . . . pourpres . . . ivresses pénitentes . . . strideurs étranges . . .silances traversés des Mondes et des Anges." This list may be supplemented by a few concrete nouns in the plural. Spitzer (1969) suggests that in Racine's poetry, for example, the plural is one of several "muting devices." In describing this muting effect, Spitzer uses such expressions as "those contour blurring plurals of abstractions," "the plural is weakening the sensuous content: the indefinite plural blurs the sensuous outline of the image" (ibid., 127), or, "by the plural the physical aspect is somewhat concealed" (ibid., 128). Elsewhere I have suggested that this muting effect of the plural depends on

> the cognitive differentiation of information into a unique, stable item, and a "regression" to a less differentiated mode of cognition, effected by a multiplicity of items preventing each other from usurping our attention. Thus, the muting use of the plural may be regarded as a moderate version of "thing-destruction," where no "thing-free," or even "gestalt-free" qualities are generated, only what might be called "blurred gestalts." (Tsur, 1983a: 33; also Tsur, 1992, chapter 21)

Thus, Rimbaud's massive (and unusual) use of plural nouns may be regarded as another stage in the transition from hard-and-fast objects to the flux of gestalt-free qualities. But one of the most decisive contributions to the overwhelming thing-free vision of the sonnet is to be attributed to the series of vowels modified by the color adjectives. *A*, or *E*, or *I*, or *U*, or *O* have a certain systematic ambiguity. They may refer to an abstract phonetic category, or to certain streams of acoustic energy spread over bands of specified frequencies (some critics of this poem would add a third possibility: the graphemes signifying the abstract phonetic categories). It should also be noted that colors too are streams of (visual) energy. In chapter 2, I summarized Rakerd's (1984) experiments according to which vowels are more linguistically perceived in consonantal context than in isolation, and, conversely, perceptual features are more readily perceived in isolated vowels than in consonantal context. Rimbaud's "Voyelles" is one of the very few (perhaps the only major) poem in the major Western languages in which isolated vowels are systematically presented to the reader's perception. When isolated vowels are qualified by color adjectives, the vowels may be perceived as thing-free streams of (acoustic) energy, the impact of which may be enhanced by some thing-free stream of (visual) energy—at least in certain conditions when the directly perceived acoustic information and the semantic information referring to the visual domain are perceived as if somehow they were interacting. My conception of this poem is founded, then, on a radical shift of the focus from the coupling of specific vowels with specific colors to the verbal devices that may jointly evoke an overall thing-free vision and to the kind of performance in which this may occur.

We have, then, a highly generalized explanation of the effect that isolated vowels qualified by color adjectives may have in certain thing-free contexts. We still need to account for the specific coupling of certain vowels with certain colors. One of the most popular explanations is the "colored spelling book" theory, according to which Rimbaud's poem reflects the association of specific vowels with specific colors in his childhood spelling book. Even if the existence of such a spelling book is proved beyond doubt, this explanation's most conspicuous flaw is that the genetic fallacy lurks behind it. It explains what it is that may have suggested precisely those associations to Rimbaud, but not why a poem based on them has aroused such public interest for over a century. In other words, it explains at best why these associations occurred to Rimbaud, but not why other people (except those who learned to read from the same spelling book) may find them meaningful. A second flaw is that the explanation is based on too crude a conception of the poet's psychology (the coarsest version of the conditioned reflex) and leaves very little to his creative imagination. Rimbaud himself, at any rate, tended to regard the issue in a different light: "I have invented the color of the vowels" (quoted by Plessen, 1967: 301n., and passim).

The colors of the alleged spelling book may, of course, have intersubjective validity if they reflect certain intersubjectively valid regularities. In this case, however, the spelling book theory becomes completely redundant. If some intersubjective foundation of colored hearing can be shown to exist, and to correspond to Rimbaud's combination of vowels with colors, then one need not appeal to the alleged spelling book. Étiemble (1968) and Plessen in his footsteps argue that such an intersubjective foundation for colored hearing underlying Rimbaud's sonnet is highly unlikely. Étiemble has collected many poems that may have influenced or imitated Rimbaud's poem; they seem far from agreeing which vowel goes with which color.

Now this kind of proof is anything but conclusive. It may well be the case that all the other poems are wrong, and only Rimbaud's has hit upon the psychologically valid relationship. After all, Rimbaud's poem is the only one of its kind that has earned a worldwide reputation. In other words, there may be—in fact, there seems to be—a "genuine colored hearing" verifiable on independent grounds in extra-literary reality. We have now some fairly well established knowledge about genuine colored hearing. Jakobson (1968) characterized some of the principles behind it:

> Obviously, both series of qualities, LIGHTNESS~DARKNESS and CHROMATIC~ACHROMATIC, are common to sound and visual sensations, and the structure of sound and color systems show marked agreements.
>
> Moreover, cases of pronounced colored hearing, especially in children or retained from childhood, in which acoustic impressions and particularly speech sounds "appear bound nonarbitrarily, regularly, and consistently with the same color experiences," show the close connection of the vowels /o/ and /u/ with the specifically dark colors, and of /e/ and /i/, on the other hand, with the specifically light colors. A distinct inclination to connect

the more chromatic vowels with the variegated colors /a/ with red, and, conversely, the vowels /u/ and /i/ with the black~white series is also apparent in colored hearing.

And again:

One may compare, in addition, the "agnosia for colors other than red, black and white" . . . with the stage of the single, most chromatic vowel and the splitting of consonants into labial and dental. (ibid., 84)

We also have a detailed account based on introspection of a highly perceptive and intelligent young woman, followed by Jakobson's comments based on an interview with her (see Reichard et al., 1949) and much more (see also Jakobson and Waugh, 1979: 128ff; 188ff.). But, unfortunately for the interpreter, the color-vowel pairs of "Voyelles" do not correspond to those established by extraliterary observation (mentioned, for example, by Jakobson above). Nevertheless, the general mechanisms described by Jakobson appear to form in one way or another the foundation of our inclination to accept Rimbaud's analogies between vowels and colors. Furthermore, Jakobson and Waugh (ibid., 194) remark: "What must be avoided is the mixture of these usual ways of translating from the speech sounds to the color level with literary declarations often strained and deliberately made *á rebours*," and they quote Rimbaud's sonnet.

A more ad hoc explanation is offered by Chadwick. It takes as its point of departure "the only fact we know 'absolutely for sure'—that Rimbaud was a *poet* and that the sonnet 'Voyelles' is a poem" (1960: 27). But he, too, seems to ask the question, "Why did Rimbaud pair precisely these vowels, with these colors, in this order?" rather than "Given the sonnet in its present form, what is its likely effect on the reader?" That is, Chadwick also sets out to tell us the "naissances latentes" of the sonnet, using more linguistically relevant material than some of his predecessors, but still concerned with the poet's intention rather than with the poem as an aesthetic object. J. P. Houston summed up Chadwick's argument concerning the first line as follows:

A is *noir* because the adjective contains that vowel sound; E is *blanc* as a contrast to *noir*. I is *rouge* because *bleu* or *vert* would make either a disagreeable alliteration or a pun (hiver). O is *bleu* to avoid the pun *overe* and thus *vert* is left for U. The last two vowels are inverted to avoid a hiatus (*bleu-U*). The author notes that *jaune* and *brun* are

much rarer in Rimbaud's poetry than the colors used in "Voyelles."
(1963: 63)

Though quite a few of Chadwick's arguments can be used in a non-intentionalist interpretation, I have two objections to this kind of argumentation. First, Chadwick's approach is *prescriptive in retrospect*: this is the best result to arrive at; this is the best way to join the elements (and, presumably, these are the best elements to be given). It does not seem to allow the poet very great freedom to choose or otherwise join his elements in a good poem. I shall propose, instead, a *descriptive* approach: these are the elements, this is how they may interplay, this is what potentially is realized by the reader. Second, while some relationships pointed out by Chadwick are perceptually there in the poem (such as *noir* contains the [a] sound, or white is the sharpest contrast to black), the "rejected" possibilities appear to explain Rimbaud's possible considerations rather than the reader's perceptions. What is more, I can see no reason why a post-Romantic poet should make efforts to avoid puns. They are quite prevalent in the line of poetry stemming from Baudelaire. Consider, for instance, the following line from Baudelaire's "Au Lecteur":

Le sein martirisé d'une antique catin,

where *sein* (followed by *martirisé*) constitutes a pun with *saint*, meaning "the martyrized breast (saint) of an ancient whore."

As for the rest of the sonnet, Chadwick puts forward (pp. 33ff.) a sort of principle of multiple causation: one cannot account for the structure of this sonnet by any single hypothesis. He realizes, as well, the possible metaphorical relationship between the vowels and images associated with them: "If one proceeds now to an attentive examination of the images attached by Rimbaud to the diverse colors, one realizes that each series groups itself around one emotion. That is to say, that such images are related to such colors, not directly, but by the mediation of the emotion associated with this color" (1960: 34).

Satisfactory as this interpretation is, as far as it goes, it still falls short of realizing the multiple relationship between the various elements. The structuralist conception of this poem, formulated by Lévi-Strauss and Gérard Genette, is closely related to the conception of analogies expounded in chapter 1 (and passim). One obvious merit is that it does not impose some concrete accordance of specific vowels with specific colors, but sets out with a more abstract conception of some general correspondence between the color system and the vowel system of a language that eventually creates the illusion of the specific correspondences between vowels and colors. Lévi-Strauss (quoted by Boon, 1972: 1) writes:

> The search for correspondences of this sort is not a poet's game or a department of mystification as people have dared to say of Rimbaud's *sonnet des voyelles*: that sonnet is now indispensable to the student of language who knows the basis, not of the color phenomena, for this varies with each individual, but of the relation which unites one phenomenon to another and comprises a limited gamut of possibilities. These correspondences offer the scholar an entirely new terrain, and one which may still have rich yields to offer.

Genette gives a more detailed account of the same idea:

> The partisans of phonetic expressiveness, like Jespersen or Grammon, have attempted to attribute to each phoneme its own suggestive value said to influence in every language the composition of certain words. Others have shown the fragility of these hypotheses and concerning especially the color of vowels, the comparative tables provided by Étiemble show in a peremptory manner that the partisans of *audition colorée* do not agree upon a single attribution. Their opponents naturally conclude that *audition colorée* is nothing but a myth. . . . But the disagreement of individual tables does not ruin their validity all in all, and structuralism may propose here an interpretation that keeps account, at once, of the arbitrariness of each vowel-color correspondence and of the widespread feeling of a vocalic chromatism: it is true that no vowel in isolation naturally evokes a color; but it is also true that the distribution of colors in the spectrum . . . can find its correspondence in the distribution of the vowels in a given language: hence the idea of a table of correspondence, variable in its details but constant in its function: there is a spectrum of vowels as there is a spectrum of colors, the two systems evoke and attract each other, and the global homology creates the illusion of a term-by-term analogy. (1966: 151–52)

A similar conception of correspondences forms the foundation of the present work, and, I believe, Lévi-Strauss and Genette have put their finger on a principle that may explain an important aspect of acceptance of the VOWEL-COLOR correspondence in Rimbaud's sonnet. The main difference between our approaches lies in their lack of any attempt to work out the details of how these correspondences—or the overall correspondence of the two spectra—may contribute to the poem as a poem. In fact, Lévi-Strauss makes it quite clear that he is documenting Structuralism rather than explaining the poem, whereas I conceive of the correspondences as only one—though very important—constituent of a poem of a certain aesthetic quality.

We must distinguish, then, three kinds of explanation for the association of vowels and colors. The first is *genetic*. What is it that made Rimbaud think of precisely these associations (for example, the spelling book theory, some versions of the alchemy theory, as well as the theories relying on the shapes of letters). The second is *rhetoric*. What makes the reader accept these associations (I include here both Jakobson's and Genette's varieties of Structuralist explanation). The third is *semantic*. What specific meanings stem from attributing certain colors to certain vowels. I do not include the various "concealed message" theories (as, for example, the blazon of the female body) in any of these, although they can be forced into any one of them with some goodwill. The ensuing close reading focuses on the second and third kinds of explanation. As for the rhetoric explanation, Genette suggests that we are inclined to accept the color system and the vowel system as somehow analogous. Jakobson points out that this inclination has its origin at a very early stage of cognitive development. I shall have some remarks on the influence of poetic structure on this inclination. As a start for a semantic explanation, we may take Ullman's statement (1966: 148): "A famous example is Rimbaud's synaesthetic 'Voyelles,' where he attributes colors to the different vowels and compares them to a wide variety of objects," if we interpret *attributes* slightly out of context as "metaphorical attribution" of one thing to another, apparently unrelated with it in extraliterary reality (as opposed to another formulation in the same book "and Rimbaud actually wrote a sonnet on the color of vowels" [ibid., 86]).

The apparently disconnected nature of vowels, colors, and images is crucial in metaphorical attribution. On the other hand, certain factors urge us to bind together all these discordant elements *in spite of their incompatibility*. So far as the urge is derived from vogue or extravagance, a poem cannot be said to have aesthetic integrity. The greater the part that multiple relationship plays in perceiving the poem as a whole, the greater the literary excellence—independent of fashion—that can be attributed to it. No doubt vogue and extravagance have a fair share in most readers' willingness to suspend their disbelief about this poem, but one may not ignore the many repetitive elements that heighten the poem's unity.

No criteria can be given to name the sufficient conditions for success-fully *fusing* the logically or empirically unrelated elements. The only thing that can be said at this stage is that multiple relationship seems to have much to do with a successful fusion. What remains are a fairly large number of readers baffled by this illogical attribution of colors to speech sounds, while they feel some mysterious inner justification for doing so, or even some mysterious law or necessity lurking behind the utterly illogical surface.

We have already met one integrating factor when quoting from Genette on the overall homology between the vowel system and the color system of a language (reinforced by Jakobson's developmental comments). In addition, as suggested by Genette, the global homology creates the *illusion* of a term-by-term analogy, which the trained reader may attempt to construe—whether consciously or not—as meaning-ful metaphorical statements by, for example, finding out connotations common to the two incongruous elements. But it should be emphasized that no single cohesive factor can account for aesthetic integrity. The more unifying elements one finds, the more willing one is to suspend disbelief—despite the basic incongruence of elements. One (though in itself insufficient) incentive to seek coherence in the incongruous elements is the mere fact that the attribution occurs in a formally orga-nized discourse, a sonnet. One other important cohesive factor has been pointed out by J. P. Houston (1963: 63–64): "'Voyelles' is ar-ranged as a kind of apocalyptic crescendo in which evil yields to good. It has the pattern of a Great Chain of Being. . . . The lower life of the flies gives place to that of men, . . . with their tents and kings and then presented as violently emotional beings. . . . Finally knowledge ushers in a vision of divinity, which is at the top of the hierarchy of creation."

In the first line, one unifying factor is the rhythmic recurrence of phrases, each comprising a vowel and a color adjective:

A noir, E blanc, I rouge, U vert, O bleu.

That is, each phrase is different from the others, but on a higher level of abstraction, exactly the same pattern keeps recurring (unity in diver-sity).

There seems to be a consistent inner logic in the choice of colors, very familiar from the works of painters who obey it even when not con-scious of it. There are colors that, if mixed, yield white. Such colors are called *complementary*. Painters achieve an impact of integrity, or unity in variety, by balancing complementary colors. Whereas white is the sum of *all* colors of the spectrum, black is its opposite as the *lack* of light or color. This principle underlies the pattern of colors in this first line. It begins with black, next comes its opposite, next come red, green, blue, in the order of their place in the spectrum. The complementary color of red is an admixture of green and blue (see Arnheim, 1967: 349). In other words, the colors, even though as adjectives to vowels they serve as distracting elements, have an integrating impact in their relation to each other. *Genetically* speaking, this may mean that the graphic composition of the alleged spelling book determined the color composition of Rimbaud's sonnet. *Rhetorically* speaking, Rimbaud's colors appeal to the reader's artistic training, or, possibly, to some of his most basic physiological or psychological responses to colors—inducing him to voluntary cooperation in reproducing the sonnet. Such an interpretation is not concerned with the question of *why* these colors rather than others, but, given the colors, *what* is the relationship between them. Similarly, but to a lesser extent, the sequence of vowels in the first line may have some integrative effect, the first three coming in their order in the alphabet. The phrases in the first line are syntactically ambiguous: they may be conceived as vocative or exclamatory. In either case, linguistically they are what Jakobson (1980: 22) called *immediate signals*.

> These particular ingredients of current discourse, listed loosely, without consistent delimitation, as interjections, exclamations, and ejaculations, stand outside the general syntactic patterning of language, and they are neither words nor sentences. . . . It is characteristic that these zero parts of speech get easily misinterpreted or simply lost by subjects with a fully active left but simultaneously inactivated right hemisphere. (ibid., 22–23)

This intimate association of such phrases with the right hemisphere of the brain may account for their affective impact. At any rate, they reinforce the factors that induce the reader to a willing suspension of disbelief or, even more, to an active cooperation.

We have seen in chapter 1 that the sibilants can be pronounced in such a way that they may imitate noises or have a hushing quality. Now it is quite clear that you cannot voice an /i/ in such a way that it should sound as red as possible. What you *may* do is isolate in both sound and color some comparable features such as the *acute* quality of /i/ (as opposed to *grave*), and/or the fact that it is the *highest* of vowels, and find them analogous to the fact that red is the most intense of colors. The word *rouge* is connected with /i/ in an additional way. Although the vowels *ou* and *i* are contrasted in their ROUNDED~UNROUNDED features, they are similar in their aperture (the narrowest or highest vowels, the least chromatic ones). Another link of *rouge* to the sonnet is, in retrospect, the repetition of all its sounds (in a reversed order) at the caesura of the next line in *jour*.

The available data on "genuine colored hearing" show that /a/ is usually associated with red and not with black (although in the case reported by Reichard et al. it has been associated with tan). As I have suggested, /a/ might be associated with black as an *extreme* (not as the dark, but the chromatic extreme, in which dark and light lie undifferentiated).[1] Still, black and red are intersubjectively associated by virtue of "the preference for black and red at the stage of child development in which variegated colors are not yet distinguished" (Jakobson, 1968: 84). In addition, as Chadwick has pointed out, a short /a/ is heard in the diphthong of *noir*. All this may increase the reader's willingness to accept the attribution of *black* to /a/ and of red to /i/, even though there is nothing inherently black about /a/ or red about /i/. It is the reader who, without being aware, possibly abstracts and stresses some common features (this is what we may mean by the *interplay of sound and color*). But to do this is legitimate (aesthetically) only if there are additional integrating elements. The fact that one's awareness cannot be fully directed at all these elements at the same time and that we perceive them in spite of an overall baffling combination contributes to the mysterious impression of the sonnet. This impression is enhanced by the tenor of the metaphor in line 2. *Latentes* indicates some dormant quality, present but not fully actualized. "Je dirai . . . vos naissances latentes," on the other hand, suggests the translation of an essence into a temporal sequence: actualized in the past but not fully revealed. This interpretation, fluctuating between the two possibilities, may reinforce the actualization of subtle analogies and relationships in line 1, as suggested.

One could further speculate on the impressionistic admixture of elements, in analogy with painting techniques. There is a very sharp contrast between the high /i/ and the low /a/. There is an equally sharp

---

1. This capability of *seeing* both /a/ and black *as* the extremes of some scale, and analogous as such, seems akin to th ecapability of understanding "the request to pronounce the word *till* and to mean it as a verb" (Wittgenstein, 1976: 214ᵉ).

contrast between black and white. These contrasts, however, do not focus the reader's attention. Instead, they diffuse it. Whereas *black* is attributed to /a/, *white* is not attributed to its opposite, but to French *e*, which is a rather colorless (that is, intermediate) vowel. It is pronounced with the tongue in an intermediate position, neither low as /a/, nor high as /i/ or /u/; it also clearly avoids the contrast of grave and acute (è and é), or of rounded and unrounded. White, in turn, is an ambiguous color, as Rudolf Arnheim (1967: 352) pointed out: "White is completeness and nothingness. Like the shape of the circle, it serves as a symbol of integration without presenting to the eye the variety of vital forces that it integrates, and thus is as complete and empty as a circle. Not so the complementary colors. They show completeness as the balance of opposites." If so, there is, similar to impressionistic painting, a most intensive use of contrasting colors, while nevertheless the contrasts are blurred by diffusion.

Line 3 begins with the same two words as line 1. Their grammatical relationship, however, has changed. Whereas in line 1 *noir* is an epithet of /a/, in line 3 it is an epithet of *corset*, an apposition to /a/, being a nonemphatic reminder of the blackness of /a/. Subsequently, the quatrain exploits *blackness*, and the reader refers it to /a/ only by remembering that it is "essentially" black. *Flies* are black, *cruelty* is frequently associated with black, and *ombre* too develops a further aspect of *black*. The scene implies enormous, violent energy by "éclatantes . . . bombinent . . . cruelles" (if the brilliant connotations of éclatantes is shown to be relevant, it enhances the fusion of incongruous senses and colors). Line 3 suggests a sensuous metaphor: flies are black, and when they *surround* something they "look like" a black corset. *Velu* (velvety) may primarily refer to the fine, almost microscopic but thick "hair" of the flies, enhancing the impression of subtle visual discerning, but at the same time it may impart an undifferentiated tactile sensation to the whole. *Éclatantes*, on the other hand, referring to the overall impression of suddenly flying apart, implies that no attention is paid to the individual flies (in other words, the image simultaneously presents a more than usually minute observation and a more than usually vague overall impression, while *velu* in its visual and tactile aspects contributes to both). The spiritual adjective *cruelles*, qualifying—and incompatible with—*puanteurs*, amplifies two attributes of the noun: great violence and intense displeasure. Being an attribute of some stinking object, *puanteurs* is an abstract noun replacing an indefinite concrete noun. It is not only a very intense, thing-free quality, but also introduces, quite unexpectedly, the tactile sense, and in a high tension. *Puanteurs* presses with extreme violence to all sides (reinforced by *éclatantes*) against the corset, whereas the corset presses *from* all directions, but instead of a solid body, it encounters the resistance of intense "stenches." *Bombinent*, on the one hand, reinforces the implications of *éclatantes* (by connoting explosion); on the other hand, it refers to an almost contradictory activity. Whereas the latter suggests flies collectively flying apart, the former marks vigorous assaults of individual flies toward the center.

E has been assigned to the color white. In line 5 we again meet this vowel, but not before the word *blancs* recurs at the second hemistich of line 6. In the meantime, whiteness is connoted by white things, such as *glaciers*, or by an abstraction like *candeurs*. Candor is a moral virtue, usually associated with whiteness. Latin *candidus* means "white, sincere," and its etymology suggests "radiance, purity." *Vapeur* is in harmony with trends of post-Romantic poetry, which, as noticed by Josephine Miles (1965: 42, 47), is inclined to bestow on objective *scene* terms such as *wind* what Wordsworth would present as the motion of spirit, with *breath* as its main object. In this context, one may consider *vapeurs* as quite significant, especially with a nominalized predicate: *candeurs des*. . . . We are obviously in the realm of intense, thing-free qualities.

One might well imagine Baudelaire, for instance, using *vapeurs* in connection with some poisonous exhalation. Consequently, one should not say that *vapeurs* and *tentes* illustrate in some way *candeurs*, but rather that *candeurs* and *vapeurs* and *tentes* elucidate each other. These latter give "body" and possibly place to "airy nothing," whereas the former specifies what kind of vapors and tents we are requested to imagine. Unlike the "tents of Kedar," these should be imagined as white, and the vapors must have some refreshing quality, such as vaporescent dew at dawn rather than mist or fog (that connote dark and dullness).

Three potentials of *glaciers* have been emphasized in this sonnet: their sheen and whiteness (by association with *candeurs*), their "proud" stature (*fiers*), and their shape (of lances). All these, in turn, can be detached from *glaciers*, and together with *tentes* be associated with *rois blancs*. Associating these items with *rois blancs* and *glaciers* should present them as fluctuating, thing-free qualities and prevent the reader from drawing unambiguous conclusions (such as J. P. Houston's single-minded discovery "of their primitive simplicity with their tents and kings"). *Frissons d'ombelles*, too, transfers attention from the thing to its aspect: the delicate vibrations.

When discussing line 1, I have suggested there might be some correspondence, or rather interplay, between *e* and whiteness. The intermediate position of this vowel possibly emphasizes that aspect of white which has been described by Rudolf Arnheim as "completeness and nothingness." In line 5 the sound *e* emphatically recurs in *cand**eurs** des vap**eurs***; the shift of pronunciation is like that from *de* to *deux*. The "radiance" connotation of *candeur* and the acute, light feature of **-eur** mutually enhance each other. As suggested in chapter 2 (in my discussion of phonological universals), the sound sequence **-eur** and nasal vowels may have special affective powers in nonreferential use. Accordingly, it might be illuminating to notice this shift from *e* to **-eurs** (and, likewise, in lines 12 and 14 from oral *o* to a nasalized *õ*, occurring in the words *Clair**on*** and *ray**on***).

Lines 7 and 8 again present violent emotional response. "I, pourpres" reminds the reader that in line 1 this vowel was described as "rouge." We have also observed in chapter 3 that phonetically /i/ was the highest and sharpest of vowels, whereas red is physically the color of the longest wave in the spectrum that has a heightening effect on blood circulation. It is the warmth correlated to this heightening effect that mediates between *red* and the violent emotional responses in these lines.[2] This may account for the pairing of *pourpres* with *colère*. Similarly, both *ivresse* and *rire* connote intense emotional responses. *I* is the vowel in *rire* and in the sound of laughter *hi-hi-hi*. As we shall see in chapter 4, the consonant *r* is apt to become expressive in a context of violence; in line 7 there are six /r/ sounds, as against 1 to 4 (an average of 2 to 3) in the other lines. *Pourpres* (especially in the plural) evokes a thing-free quality variously bearing on the subsequent images: it is the color of vomited blood, of the beautiful lips, and, possibly, of the wine causing the drunkenness. Drunkenness may have caused vomiting as well as the outburst of laughter (but we may not determine one fixed relationship). Both vomiting and laughter evoke the same kinesthetic image of spasmodic pushing out. Choler and penitence are two alternative ways a drunkard behaves. *Ivresse* may refer either to high spirits

2. The relationship between body warmth and emotional arousal appears to be deeply rooted in human biology. "The morpheme for *hot* stands for rage in Hebrew, enthusiasm in Chinese, sexual arousal in Thai, and energy in Hausa. However, this disagreement does not suggest the operation of accidental factors since there is an undoubted kinship in the range of meanings. All seem to involve heightened activity and emotional arousal. No case was discovered in which the morpheme for *hot* named a remote, calm (in fact *cool*) manner" (Brown, 1968: 146).

resulting from excessive drinking, or to some heightened spiritual experience, possibly involving some real penitence. What is characteristic
of these two lines, then, is, first, a high degree of unity by analogy and
by possible metonymic relationships; second, intense bodily images;
third, violent human responses.

French *u* (/ü/), according to Jakobson's analysis, may have sheen,
as contrasted with, say, the grave *ou* (/u/) or the chromatic /a/. This
distinctive feature, shapeless and meaningless in itself, suggests, when
paired with *calm*, some sort of *serenity*. *Cycles*, detached from all context
has, nevertheless, some resemblance of shape with the rounded /u/
or /ü/, as well as with the vibrations of the seas. As Arnheim's analysis indicates, a circle may have the structural qualities of balance and
completeness. "Vibrements divins des mers" suggests calm. Actually,
it implies the negation of the opposite of calm: there are no powerful
waves, there are fine vibrations. *Vibrements* in relation with *mers* suggests
cycles; they also suggest the shape of wrinkles mentioned in the next
line. *Pâtis* suggests greenness, *virides* suggests bluish-green; the latter
connotes serenity, the former—pastoral calm. Green and blue are near
the short-wave end of the spectrum. They are, biologically and psychologically, the least agitating colors. All this, of course, gets particular
validity from the explicit meaning of *paix* (emphasized by repetition
and alliteration with *pâtis*). *Grands fronts* suggests an intellectual quality
reinforced by *studieux*; in the present context it may even imply some
philosophic peace or serenity. Alchemy may print wrinkles on the studious brows magically, as it were, or metonymically: as a result of long
study, wrinkles may be printed on one's forehead.

One should not, it seems to me, "take the hint" from *alchemy* and seek
the clue for the poem in occult lore. But *l'alchimie* does perceptually contribute to the sonnet; it enhances the impression that substances have
here changed essences, that they have been mysteriously turned into
each other.

Unlike the famous blind man who associated the color scarlet with
the sound of the trumpet, Rimbaud associated the clarion's sound with
the sound /o/, which, in turn, was associated in line 1 with blue. There
is here, apparently, some contradiction: one may associate the sounds
of very similar instruments with a color of short wavelength as well
as with one of the longest wavelength. In fact, it seems to prove my
previous contention that far from responding to some preestablished
common attributes, the reader in his imagination is inclined to select
and emphasize, after the event, the relevant attributes.

In the first line, /o/ is associated with the color blue; in the last tercet it is associated with violet (which is a color closely associated with blue). This is somewhat odd because there is a very widespread (presumably intercultural) intuition that the rounded back vowels are dark. Here it seems that the /o/ is associated through the rounded shape of lips (or grapheme) with the shape of the opening of the instrument, whereas the instrument is related to blue through the sheen of its sound. At the same time, the sound of the clarion is associated, of all things, with *silences*, constituting an oxymoron. *Plein des* as a preposition merely relates the sound to the instrument. Yet it contributes to the quality of the sound's *fullness*. *Étranges* renders *strideurs* mysterious, otherworldly, while it retains its compelling though confused quality (possibly moderating the connotations of unpleasantness). When the reader comes on *silences*, the oxymoron rejects all the audible qualities of *Clairon*, abstracting and amplifying the other ones; these, in turn, fuse with *silences* and qualify it. The most prominent ones are the intense otherwordliness and a thick quality of fullness applying now to *silences* too. *Blue* is called up by a unique combination of attributes implying a serene sky. ***Clair**on* includes (and is etymologically derived from) *clair*, reinforcing the clear blue sky and, indeed, players of brass instruments characterize it not only as "bright," but even as "dazzling" like the sun. This perceived quality of the clarion's sound appears to qualify the blue associated with the vowel /o/ as bright and shiny rather than dark blue (reinforced by *rayon violet* in the last line). *Traversés* reinforces the "clear and piercing" connotations of the clarion's sound. Worlds and Angels, too, are usually associated with Sky or Heaven. This implies an additional oxymoron, that the transparent, "nonsubstantial" silence, or blue, is replete, or crisscrossed, with worlds, or angels, or their footsteps.

One interesting aspect of the clarion here is that it is "full of stridors" (*stridor* meaning "a harsh grating or creaking sound"). Unlike much nineteenth-century poetry indulging in "sweet soft music," this sonnet attempts to assimilate harsh *strideur* (as, in the first stanza, *puanteurs*). The sound is relatively thing-free as compared to the instrument that produced it. Rimbaud's phrase, on the other hand, further directs attention away from the sound to one of its perceived attributes, its stridors (in the plural). This phrasing may be highlighted by comparing it to Oliver Bernard's plain prose translation of the phrase in the Penguin Poets *Rimbaud*: "full of strange piercing sounds." Bernard focuses attention on the sounds characterized as "strange and piercing." The

French original focuses attention on the "stridors" (the "piercingness"), which quality is amplified and its independence emphasized by the adjective *étranges*.

What effect is produced by these "strange stridors" in the poem? Why does Rimbaud prefer the stridor of the clarion to its sound proper? It seems that the stridors contribute some mysterious quality to the perception that is rendered in the sound itself as somehow less prominent. Let us consider the possible referent of the phrase. In a context discussing thing-free and gestalt-free qualities it may be suggested that in music the sounds are the thing, whereas the overtones when perceived as detached from the fundamental are perceived as thing-free. When a greater than usual number of overtones is perceived in the brasses, it may influence the perceived quality in several respects. First, a thing-free aura can be perceived; this aura may also be responsible for the "dazzling brightness" mentioned. Second, owing to the excessive number of overtones, the sounds of the brass instruments are sometimes perceived as having a "rough surface." When I asked a brass player about the *strideurs* of the clarion, he at first did not know what I was talking about; but as soon as I translated it as "a harsh grating quality," he related it, straightaway, to the excess of overtones. This effect becomes especially perceptible when the overtones do not fuse into a background texture.

> It is difficult, if not impossible, to imagine a visual figure without also imagining the more continuous, homogeneous ground against which it appears. But in "aural space," in music, there is no given ground; there is no necessary, continuous stimulation, against which all figures must be perceived. The only thing that is continuous in aural experience is unorganized, timeless silence— the absence of stimulation whatsoever. (Meyer, 1956: 186)

When the full body of a brass instrument's sound, the fundamental together with the "rough surface" of "grating" overtones, disrupts the continuity of silence, it is sometimes perceived as if it "broke in" from "nowhere"; and the undifferentiated, precategorical grating overtones have a decisive part in this effect. The metaphorical effect of this "irruption" is sometimes a feeling that behind the silence there could be some enormous, full worlds, from which the sounds burst into one's perceptual field.

O at the beginning of lines 12 and 14 has a "systematic ambiguity."

Functioning simultaneously in first and second order language, it is perceived both as the name of a vowel and as an interjection. The second possibility amplifies the emotional impact of the whole sonnet and enhances our interpretation of the phrase series as exclamatory (considered in connection with the first line).

The last line has a strong impact of *finality* for several reasons. It deviates from the previous lines in that it contains the only explicitly exclamatory phrase; *Oméga* (the last letter in the Greek alphabet) connotes a final stage. This is possibly one of the reasons for changing the order of /u/ and /o/ in line 1. *Ses Yeux* (his/her eyes) is frequently interpreted as God's eyes, the supreme being, the last in the sequence from the smallest and lowest beings (flies) to the largest and highest one (although some critics maintain that it was Rimbaud's mother who was his Alpha and Omega). *Suprême* in line 12 comes to mean, first, high (in the sky or Heaven); second, majestic; third, wonderful; and fourth, final. *Clairon*, capitalized, with the epithet *suprême*, related to Angels (also capitalized) and God, may suggest the Last Judgment. Of the second tercet, dealing with /o/ and *blue*, line 14 is the first to mention the color. *Violet rays*, visible light of the shortest wavelength, form the *end* of the spectrum. They may refer here to the *blue* of the eyes and to the azure of the sky as well.

In nonpoetical discourse, sound repetition is either likely to pass unnoticed or to yield a jingle. In poetical discourse, it may be an *additional* factor in multiple relationship. It seems to me that in "Voyelles" the sound repetition contributes to multiple relationship. Some kind of sound repetition may in sharp focus impress the reader as ingenuity, whereas in soft focus (divergent style) the same kind of repetition is perceived as fusing in a smooth, musical texture. Consider George Herbert's echo poem "Heaven."

> O, who will show me those delights on high?
> > ECHO: *I.*
> Thou Echo, thou art mortal, all men know.
> > ECHO: *No.*
> Wert thou not born among the trees and leaves?
> > ECHO: *Leaves.*
> And are there any leaves that still abide?
> > ECHO: *Bide.*
> What leaves are they? impart the matter wholly.
> > ECHO: *Holy.*

Are holy leaves the Echo, then, of bliss?
ECHO: *Yes.*
Then tell me, what is that supreme delight?
ECHO: *Light.*
Light to the mind: what shall the will enjoy?
ECHO: *Joy.*
But are there cares and business with the pleasure?
ECHO: *Leisure.*
Light, joy, and leisure; but shall they perséver?
ECHO: *Ever.*

Echo is a repetition of sounds where there are two rhyming words, the second is wholly included in the first, as *light* in *delight*, or *leisure* in *pleasure*. When, as in Herbert's poem, the word *echo* draws attention to the sound repetition, it is perceived as a witty play on words. What strikes the reader is that a similar device in "Voyelles" fuses in a pleasant, harmonious texture, yielding musicality rather than intellectual play. There is only one pair of rhyming words in this sonnet, neither wholly included in the other: *voyelles* and *cruelles*. As for the rest, *latentes* is included in *éclatentes*, *tentes* in *pénitentes*, *latentes* and *éclatentes*; *belles* is included in *ombelles*, *rides* in *virides*, *yeux* in *studieux*, and *Anges* in *étranges*. One may point out three relevant differences between these two poems: (1) in French this device is far more natural than in English; (2) in Herbert's poem the echoing words have been isolated and emphasized to an unusual degree, whereas in Rimbaud's poem they have been integrated syntactically as well as prosodically so that this special way of rhyming frequently passes unnoticed; (3) the focus of the English poem can be considered split and sharp on various grounds, while in the French poem images are blended to an unusual degree.

The musicality of the sonnet (which, in turn, reinforces the cohesive factors) relies on a texture of intensely repeated, diffuse sound clusters. To mention the most conspicuous: *blanc—bleu*; *blanc—naissances—latentes—éclatantes—puanteurs*;   *rouge—jour*;   *autour—puanteur*; *bombinent—ombre—ombelles*; *lances—blancs*; *lances—glaciers*; *lèvre—colère lèvres—ivresses—vibrements—divins—virides*; *strideurs—rides—virides*; *strideurs—studieux*; *strideurs—étranges*; *imprime—suprême animaux—l'alchimie imprime*.

The logical crust has been broken in "Voyelles" by the illogical metaphoric attributions and by the abolition of the subject-predicate logic of sentences. The phrase is the prevalent syntactic form. There is only one main close in it (in line 2), constructed around a finite verb. There are two other finite verbs (in lines 4 and 11), predicates in two adjectival clauses that qualify two nouns, which, in turn, form part of no sentence in the conventional sense. The general syntactic structure is phrasal and follows patterns like that in lines 7–8. Here, first, there are four apposite phrases: "I, pourpres, sang craché, rire des lèvres belles"; then, two adverbial phrases, joined by the disjunction *ou* ("Dans la colère ou les ivresses pénitantes"). This phrasal structure receives its significance from what it is *not*. One conspicuous effect of a finite verb predicate in syntactic structures is the bestowal of some definite direction on the sequence. The appositive structure of Rimbaud's sonnet, in the absence of finite verbs, lumps together images at rest before the mind's eye; one may contemplate them almost at one's leisure—that is, they do not press on toward the end of the utterance. This effect is reinforced by the fact that some of the action verbs, such as *cracher, semer, traverser*, occur in the past participle: the action denoted by them is over, and their formal topics are passive recipients of the action; the actions denoted by these verbs have become static attributes of their topics in a timeless present.

Plessen counts the sonnet form among the three major principles that can account for the structure of "Voyelles," together with the vowels and the colors. "Concerning 'Voyelles,' what conclusion can one draw from Rimbaud's utilization of the sonnet form? It appears to me that the idea of *play* must be retained and that in 'Voyelles,' as sometimes elsewhere, Rimbaud is more or less aware of the playful character of his enterprise" (1967: 297–98). As a matter of fact, I believe that the possibility that "Voyelles" is essentially playful must be taken seriously, even though in this chapter I have worked out only a highly emotional— even ecstatic—reading.

However, the sonnet form per se can be taken to support either a playful or a high-serious reading. In this sense, the sonnet form is perfectly transparent. A sonnet may exhibit any attitude. Nonetheless, the sonnet form does substantially contribute to the general effect of the poem as considered so far. But this contribution is not derived from some historical association of the sonnet form with tones or themes. Rather, it is derived from the perceptual quality resulting from an interplay between the sonnet's syntactic and the prosodic organization. I have elsewhere discussed some of the relevant issues.

J. Lever has observed that the octet of the Italian sonnet proved particularly useful for poets, owing to an ambiguity resulting from a superimposition of the stanza forms. Six out of eight lines may be grouped as quatrains and couplets. . . . This, however, is a *potential* ambiguity, usually unrealized as, e.g., in Keats's "On First Looking into Chapman's Homer"; it becomes *actual* ambiguity when reinforced by syntax, as in Milton's "On His Blindness," or in Wordsworth's "Westminster Bridge" sonnet. (Tsur, 1977: 198)

Later on, I suggest:

A strong-shaped stanza may achieve a quality of sharpness, of wit, "the psychological atmosphere of certainty, of patent purpose"— if one may quote Pope outrageously out of context—"with sure returns of still expected rhymes." Conversely, a stanza of weak shape, with a blurred rhyme scheme, may have a soft quality— with no sharp edges, so to speak—with a rather affective impact. (ibid., 199)

In Rimbaud's sonnet, the only place where the clear-cut stanza form is blurred is at the end of the first quatrain. In other words, if the relative clause "Qui bombinent . . . golfes d'ombre" (who bomb . . . gulfs of shadow) does locally impose some clear syntactic shape on the phrases, it is used at the same time to blur the stanza shape. But on the whole the sonnet form has two apparently opposite effects: first, it articulates to some extent, with the help of the rhyme scheme, the nearly amorphous mass of phrases (images) lumped together. With the exception of the clause run-on from the first quatrain to the second, the phrases containing images devoted to each vowel conclude either at the end or at the exact middle of a stanza. By the same token, the echoic structure of the rhyme scheme furthers the perceptual fusion of the units— prosodic, syntactic, figurative—into an emotional whole.

To conclude this reading of "Voyelles," we might link the results of the poem's detailed description with the theoretical framework derived from Bergson and Ehrenzweig to suggest an overall structure. To "the constant flux of states extending into each other," an overall pattern has been "superimposed"—the "apocalyptic crescendo" from flies to the "epiphanic Os" culminating in the "vision of divinity, which is at the top of the hierarchy of creation." Given the highly emotional, thing-free impact of the lump of percepts presented throughout the sonnet, "the vision of *divinity*" has turned into a "*vision* of divinity." On reaching the culminating point, the reader "retro-relates" it (William James's term, quoted by Ehrenzweig) with previously scattered sense perceptions so that he may perform what Ehrenzweig would call "secondary elaboration" or "superimposition" of an all-pervasive pattern.[3]

A final remark. It has sometimes been suggested that "Voyelles" is a private poem, with no sufficient public foundation. One fact, at least, runs contrary to this assumption. A fair number of readers, unaware of the extensive source-hunting literature, appear to find literary interest in the sonnet. The foregoing analysis indicates that responses are in the public domain. If there is a difference between this poem and the majority of public poems, it lies in the subtlety of distinctions to be made.

The general reader has been trained to abstract common qualities from contradictory terms and to respond to them (whether intentionally and consciously or not); he is used to comparing repeated sound clusters, which are at cross-purposes with their syntagmatic combinations. In "Voyelles" one is required to draw far subtler distinctions, not only between syntagmatic and repetitive sound combinations, but between distinctive features of one single phoneme. Furthermore, when relating vowels to irrelevant images, one is required to abstract semantic aspects, too, comparable in subtlety to distinctive features of phonemes. The question, then, is not whether the poem makes use of private or public material, but rather where to draw the line between the legitimate and illegitimate domain of poetry on the scale of subtleties. This, however, seems to me a question of minor importance.

3. I have elsewhere discussed at some length the possible cognitive mechanism underlying this "retro-relation" generating an "emotive crescendo" in poetic structure (see Tsur, 1977: 213–14; see also Tsur, 1992, chapters 18–19).

Cognitive Explanation

It is quite true that I have not been able to accept all his findings, but I still believe that one can pay no greater tribute to a scholar or scientist than to take his theories seriously and to examine them with the care they deserve.—E. H. Gombrich, *The Sense of Order*

This last chapter will mainly consider methodological problems. It will compare the relative merits of a cognitive and a psychoanalytic approach to issues related to the emotional symbolism of speech sounds. This will involve me in some disagreement with two authorities whom I regard as my masters in important respects. Against Wellek and Warren's position I shall defend the application of psychology in general, and cognitive psychology in particular, to the explanation of central issues in literature. I shall use Iván Fónagy's Freudian analysis of articulatory gestures to indicate the limitations of a Freudian approach to the emotional symbolism of speech sounds. I shall adopt Kenneth Burke's criticism of Freud's inclination toward what he calls "an essentializing strategy" and shall attempt to show that such strategies tend to penalize Freudian interpretation till this very day, even at its best. One of this book's major assumptions is that poetic effects arise from a disruption of the smooth functioning of cognitive processes. But psychopathological processes also consist of such disruptions. In the course of this chapter I shall consider at some length the relationship between aesthetic effects, psychopathological processes, and the disruption of the smooth functioning of the cognitive system. It will be suggested that both the aesthetic and the psychopathological processes cause a delay or disruption of cognitive functioning, but for very different purposes, which considerably constrain the possibility of drawing inferences from each. Many Freudian literary theorists seem to disregard these constraints. Another issue to be considered is the relationship between critical terms and the theoretical framework within which they are used. One major assumption of cognitive poetics is that the use of descriptive terms may become meaningful only within the framework of some theory or theoretical model, which is to fulfill the task of commonplaces in the rhetorical sense of the term. On the other hand, theories and models can be meaningfully applied to specific poems only via critical terms with properly articulated descriptive contents. To take a simple example: the descriptive statement "This poem has twenty three lines" may be perfectly true, but trivial. On the other hand, the statement "This poem has fourteen lines" may become significant, with reference to the sonnet model. And conversely, the sonnet model can be meaningfully applied to a specific poem only via such descriptive terms that refer to the number of lines, rhyme-scheme, etc. (This conception of the structure of the critical statement is elaborated in Tsur, 1992, chapter 21.) A brief comparison of a cognitive and a psychoanalytic discussion of the sound patterns of one poetic stanza suggests that both theories fulfill the commonplace function of theories; but psychoanalytic theory does not seem to offer terms with properly articulated descriptive contents.

The most important single attempt to account for the perceptual, emotional, and semantic values of speech sounds from the poetic as well as the psychoanalytic point of view is, I believe, Iván Fónagy's work during the past few decades. As is apparent by now, its former aspect considerably influenced the present work. The publication of Fónagy's admirable *La Vive Voix* (1983) gives me an opportunity to compare the cognitive to the psychoanalytic approach to sound symbolism.

The Rolled /r/: Essentializing vs. Proportionalizing

In light of the foregoing conception I shall look at Fónagy's discussion of the rolled /r/.

The study of neurotic symptoms and of dreams has taught us that a faint resemblance or a certain functional analogy are sufficient for an unconscious identification of one sexual organ with another. It is no coincidence, for example, that it is the phallic period during which children learn to master the rolled [r], a sound that presupposes a strong erection of the tongue. It seems as if we could take literally the metaphor of the English phonetician T. H. Pear which characterizes the non-apical pronunciation of /r/ as an "emasculation." (Fónagy, 1971: 161; see also Fónagy, 1983: 95–103)

Further, in certain circumstances, a strongly rolled /r/ may be "considered by the archaic ego as a phallic menace. It is the same gesture that we encountered in the form of an erect menacing finger" (ibid.).

Now it is perfectly clear that without some such explanation we cannot account for certain well-established literary uses of the apical /r/. Acoustically, the /r/ is continuous, periodic, sonorous, and relatively unencoded, just as all the other liquids (/l, m, n/) are. Indeed, the /r/ is employed for its sonorous quality in poems that express especially tender moods (see my discussion of Jabotinsky's Hebrew translation of Verlaine's "Chanson d'Automne," in chapter 2). Nevertheless, in onomatopoetic words the /r/ is more frequently used than the other liquids for the imitation of menacing sounds, such as thunder. Likewise, "this apical /r/ is significantly more frequent in aggressive and erotic poems than in idyllic poems by the same authors" (ibid.).[1]

Now, in spite of all the foregoing allowances, I (and some other readers) feel that the notion of "an unconscious identification of one sexual organ with another" is somehow beside the point. It is not incorrect to regard the tongue as a sexual organ; but it is, doubtless, so many things besides being a sexual organ. Thus, treating phallic erection as a (causal) ancestor of an erect menacing finger, or of the strong erection of the tongue in pronouncing the /r/ with a strong rolling, seems to be a reductionist (or, in Burke's terminology, an essentializing) strategy. It might be far more adequate—and, I believe, some practicing Freudian analysts would agree with me today—to treat phallic erection, the erect finger, and the erect tongue as concrete manifestations in their own right of a general attitude. This attitude has such ingredients as self-assertion and menace. At the same time, each erect gesture has specific ingredients not shared by the other two, such as the conspicuous sexual ingredient in phallic erection, and periodicity,

---

1. I have, nevertheless, suggested in chapter 1 a cognitive explanation of this phenomenon. /r/, although a periodic liquid, has outstanding aggressive potentials, especially in languages in which it is rolled or intermittent. It is, actually, double-edged: on the one hand, it is periodic; on the other, it is *multiply* interrupted.

sonority, and the production of an abstract phonetic entity in lingual erection. When a schoolteacher warns the kids with a lifted finger to behave well, it will rarely be considered an erotic suggestion. According to this conception, the fascinating neurotic instances quoted by Fónagy do not necessarily support the view that behind an erect tongue or finger an erect phallus is lurking, but rather that in these instances the neurotics are incapable of keeping the various manifestations of the same general attitude separate: they turn a partial identity into a complete identification.

Some methodological issues that will be considered relevant to this example are discussed in Burke's modern classic, "Freud and the Analysis of Poetry" (1957b). Burke makes a distinction between an essentializing mode of interpretation and a mode that stresses the proportion of ingredients.

> The tendency of Freud is toward the first of these. That is, if one found a complex of, let us say, seven ingredients in a man's motivation, the Freudian tendency would be to take one of these [the sexual manifestation] as the essence of the motivation and to consider the other six as sublimated variants. . . . The proportional strategy would involve the study of these [seven] as a cluster. The motivation would be synonymous with the interrelationships between them. (ibid., 224)

Burke remarks that Freud himself, interestingly enough, was originally nearer to the proportionalizing view than he later became (ibid., 227). He also suggests that the proportionalizing strategy is preferable for literary purposes. On his part, the essentializing strategy is linked with a normal ideal of science: to "explain the complex in terms of the simple."

> This ideal almost vows one to select one or another motive from a cluster and interpret the others in terms of it. . . . Now I don't see how you can possibly explain the complex in terms of the simple without having your very success used as a charge against you. When you get through, all that your opponent need say is: "But you have explained the complex in terms of the simple—and the simple is precisely what the complex is not." (ibid., 224)

When essentializing (or turning a partial identity into a complete identification) is brought to an extreme, the results are absurd indeed. Thus, for instance, a symposium participant discussing Fónagy's chapter (Chatman, 1971: 174) commented: "How can one speak of the expressive value of a glottal stop in a given language when it is a phoneme? Would Fónagy say that such a language is more aggressive than one which does not contain the glottal stop as a phoneme? This would lead to a kind of linguistic racism. . . . Could one really say that the French lost their virility when they lost their apical /r/?"

This remark reflects an oversimplified position. If you do not treat it as a parody, you have to admit that it uses an extreme essentializing strategy in the service of an opposite kind of essentializing strategy, which the speaker states as follows: "It is impossible to ascribe values to body movements without reference to the system to which they belong" (ibid.). This *appears* to reflect a proportionalizing strategy; however, it applies it rather dogmatically. It seems to be an observational fact that speech sounds do have expressive values. Or should we say so much worse for the facts? It should be clear, too, that this expressive value has little to do with the phonemic value of speech sounds. The participant, who "also found himself far from accepting the psychoanalytic analysis of Fónagy," seems to deny by the same token that some of the subphonemic perceptual information becomes, in certain circumstances, somehow relevant to the total (say, poetic) effect. To paraphrase this participant, "one must ascribe values to body movements *with reference to the deviations from* the system to which they belong." In fact, a nonreductionist way to handle poetic effects is to regard the phonemes (or other linguistic units) as simultaneously belonging to several systems. One of the basic assumptions of this book (and of cognitive poetics in general) is that it is impossible to account for the perceived effects of phonemes without going outside "the system to which they belong."

Fónagy furnishes several examples, the gist of which is that "the non-acquisition of the apical r seems to reflect an incomplete resolution of the [Oedipal] conflict" (1983: 98). To what extent does this bear testimony to the phallic character of its acquisition? Far beyond the possible clinical or developmental implications of the question, the issue at stake in cognitive poetics would be this: Is it legitimate—and if yes, to what extent—to bring the sexual element into our explanation of the perceived effects of poetry?

The foregoing conception is apparently contradicted by certain "male and female forms of speech," and the verbal taboos attached to them, in "sexually bifurcated languages." Thus, "in the U.S.S.R., when schools with Chukchee as the language of teaching were first opened, 'little girls blushed and refused to read words containing an r-sound,' because 'the use of men's pronunciation was accounted indecent for women, accustomed to replace *r* and *č* phonemes by a hushing *š*'" (Jakobson and Waugh, 1979: 210).

Apparently, such verbal taboos may be taken as direct evidence for the intimate association of the [r] with virility. Indeed, Fónagy takes them as such (1983: 101). This, however, will be the case only if we grant a certain priority to the association of virility with /r/; that is, if we assume that such an intense virility is perceived in the /r/ that in certain languages (or societies) women are forbidden to pronounce it, then they must replace it. One may imagine a reverse explanation, however. Suppose that in a certain male-dominated society there are strict rules for differentiating the behavior of men and women. Suppose, as well, that self-assertive, menacing behavior is permitted only for men (such rules are, after all, different in the degree of strictness rather than in kind from the stereotypes prevalent in our own society). If we also assume that the [r] is associated with some general attitude that has such ingredients as self-assertion and menacing behavior, it should be no surprise if the rules differentiating women's from men's behavior included a taboo prohibiting women from using [r].

On the other hand, the evidence I am aware of cannot rule out either of the possibilities that there *may* or *may not* be a causal relationship between phallic menace and the perceived hardness or the rolled apical /r/. So, in the absence of further evidence, I wish to propose the following set of considerations. First of all, let us very roughly distinguish three factors in producing the phonetic category [r]: (1) an abstract phonetic category; (2) a complex articulatory gesture; (3) a psychodynamic set of unconscious elements related to erotic impulses. Nobody seems to dispute the psychological reality and the relevance of the first two. The psychological reality of the third factor also appears to be widely admitted. What is being disputed is its relevance or irrelevance to the production of [r]. Now, supposing that the third factor is also relevant to the production of [r], we have to consider a second issue as well: how, and to what extent, do the second and third factors affect the perceived quality of the phonetic category as it appears in consciousness.

Let me say at the start that I shall not attempt to settle such questions as whether the third factor exists or is relevant to the production of /r/. However, the outcome of the considerations outlined below may strongly suggest that we can account for all the phenomena under discussion without appealing to the third factor. First, in the speech mode the perceived phonetic category is typically cut off from any precategorical information, whether articulatory, acoustic, or unconscious psychodynamic. That is why it is considered an *abstract* phonetic category. Second, in the poetic mode some of the precategorical information does reach consciousness and significantly affects the *perceived quality* (but not the basic categorical distinction) of the phonetic category. These perceived qualities determine or generate the (sometimes conflicting) aspects of the speech sounds' combinational potential (see chapter 1). Third, if the erotic factor *is* relevant to the production of the apical [r], there is no reason not to suppose that it will affect in one way or another the perceived quality of the phonetic category.

Let us suppose now that the psychodynamic set of unconscious elements associated with erotic drives is *irrelevant*. Let us also suppose that in a given text the /r/ occurs more frequently than its usual distribution in the same language and that the semantic features activate in it the acoustic features [+CONTINUOUS, +PERIODIC, +SONOROUS] as well as the articulatory feature [+ERECT TONGUE]. The latter feature may bestow on the acoustic features a hard, menacing quality. These features would determine the combinational potential of /r/. In an erotic context, the combinational potential of a hard, menacing quality combines, in an attenuated form, with what Fónagy has called "phallic menace," enhances its effect, and promotes its relative prominence among the many features of the complex context. In a stormy context, the continuous, periodic, sonorous features on the one hand, and the menacing, hard feature on the other, will combine with certain semantic features and will be perceived as a sound imitation of thunder or other menacing noises of the storm. It will be noted that in the erotic context only the perceptual quality of the articulatory gesture is abstracted and used, whereas in the stormy context both the acoustic and articulatory features are abstracted and used.

Now, suppose we consider the erotic feature as relevant to the production of /r/. In this case, all (or most) of it will be activated by the erotic context; the erotic ingredients of the contents and the erotic antecedents of the articulatory gesture will reinforce each other. However, when we turn to the stormy context, the whole of the erotic factor associated with the /r/ must be omitted; only the menacing ingredient will be abstracted from it, which will reinforce the menacing feature of the articulatory gesture; these menacing features will be associated with the acoustic features of continuity and periodicity and will be perceived in the stormy situation as the sound imitation of thunder or other rough noises. Intuitively, at least, the second possibility appears a bit labored. We do not usually feel that a cumulation of /r/s in erotic contexts gives such massive support to a perceived erotic quality; it would, for the most, be perceived as reinforcing some menacing quality if there should be any in the context. And conversely, we do not seem to feel that in a stormy context the precategorical information associated with the /r/ suffers such a massive omission. On the contrary, the precategorical elements associated with /r/ seem to be far more effective in a stormy context than in an erotic one. Thus, the assumption that unconscious elements associated with erotic drives significantly affect the production and perception of the apical /r/ in the poetic mode may be considered even counterintuitive to some extent.

Glottal and Velar Stops

A story of similar structure is told by Fónagy (1971: 160) about glottal stops. As we shall see, he repeats and elaborates the anal part of the story in connection with velar stops in his later book (1983).

> What is the relation between aggression and the contraction of the glottal sphincter? Darwin considered the emotions to be the residue of certain ancestral activities: fear represents flight, anger represents combat. Strong muscular contraction is an essential element in preparation for combat, in combat itself.
>
> The glottal stop is constituted by a specific muscular contraction, a contraction which results in a complete closure at the glottal level. The metaphor of "strangled voice" seems to contain the germ of the explanation. "Strangling" foreshadows homicide. Here we have an action which, according to the magical conception of the world, should suffice in itself to eliminate one's adversary.
>
> We must also consider the primary function of the glottal sphincter—to prevent harmful corpuscles from entering the lungs. The cough is only a glottal closure which, under high subglottal pressure, serves to eliminate these corpuscles. By extension, . . . this reflex appears as a sort of rejection, a refusal. . . . A second and equally important role played by the glottal closure is the exertion of strong pressure on the diaphragm, indirectly on the intestines. . . . The glottal stop (or hiatus) is considered by grammarians to be particularly "hard" or unpleasant. The biological functions of glottal occlusion, and the transfer of the anal libido to the glottal level seems associated with the "hard attack" of anger and hatred.

Conspicuous in this quotation is its presentation of articulatory gesture and the unconscious psychodynamic elements in a proportion that
is very different from that in his discussion of /r/. The overwhelming
bulk of these passages is devoted to articulatory gestures easily accessible to introspection. They also characterize their typical perceived
emotional qualities, anger or aggression, rejection or refusal, or, still
more abstract, he mentions Gutzman's term *Unlusteinsatz* ("attack of
displeasure"). It is only at the end, and only briefly, that he mentions the
psychoanalytical term "anal libido." The emotional qualities derived
from the articulatory gestures furnish us with descriptive terms that
refer to the combinational potential of the glottal stop, terms that can
be applied to literary texts without bringing in irrelevant information.
One of the great advantages of these emotional qualities is that they
can be directly perceived, just as we perceive that the book is red or the
tea is sweet. The appeal to Darwin or to the biological functions of the
glottal sphincter has one clear purpose (very much in line with the basic
conception of cognitive poetics): to relate the perceived quality of the
glottal stops to the articulatory gesture (both accessible to introspection). Since poems are *aesthetic* objects, that is, objects whose significant
qualities are accessible through sense perception, these *perceived* qualities of glottal stops may become conspicuous and significant parts of
the perceptual surface of a poem.

The status of anal libido is quite different. It is a theoretical construct
and refers to nothing directly perceptible. The descriptive content of
the term is virtually nil and cannot be directly applied to a poetic text.
In this connection, the terms "hard attack of anger and hatred" seem
to be little more than an exact reduplication of what has already been
said of the perceived qualities of the articulatory gestures involved. All
this, however, does not amount to a reasoned denial of the relevance
of the anal libido to the perceived qualities of glottal stops. It only may
indicate that it may be of little service in describing perceived qualities
of poetic texts; it tends to become tautological, a repetitive description and explanation. Even this does not imply that the notion of anal
libido is not serviceable in describing the perceived qualities of glottal
stops. This notion may, for instance, help to account for some heightened emotional response to texts in which glottal stops abound. But
some additional articulation of the theory is necessary to account for
the difference between texts in relation to which such heightened emotional response comes into play and which does not. In this relation,
too, Fónagy points out some occasional psychopathological disruptions

of proper functioning: "This double biological functioning of glottal stops is the basis of hysterical asthmas which have as origin an anal cathexis of the glottal sphincters" (ibid.).

Poetic Language and Psychopathology

We have seen that Fónagy adduces a great deal of evidence from psychopathology and taboo systems to support his claim that the articulatory gestures required to produce the various speech sounds are associated with a variety of unconscious drives. I have already suggested that there is at least a possibility that psychopathology does not *reveal* the underlying unconscious associations, but rather *consists in* pressing them beyond their normal limit, turning a partial identity into a complete identification. I would like to elaborate a little on this suggestion. It appears that we have hit on a more general principle underlying cognitive poetics, which concerns the relationship among the natures of poetic language, cognitive processes, and psychopathological disturbances.

In an appendix to my book *On Metaphoring*, "Poetic Language, the TOT Phenomenon, and Thing-Destruction—A Psycholinguistic Model of Poetry" (Tsur, 1987: 273–88), I discuss at length what appears to be a crucial instance of this principle. This concerns a psycholinguistic mechanism that, when it functions smoothly, allows us to retrieve from long-term memory compact configurations of phonological and semantic features called *words*. When, however, the smooth functioning of this mechanism is disturbed for some reason—when, for instance, a word is on the tip of the tongue—we have an intense, diffuse feeling that seems to contain as ingredients many, or most, or all of the phonological and semantic features that were somehow prevented from growing together into the one specific word. Only the diffuse presence of these features can explain the fact that people in the TOT state are capable of producing similar-sounding words and similar-meaning words, as well as much other information. All this information may lead, eventually, to the recall—or, at least, to the recognition—of the word. That is why the absence of this word is experienced as a *unique* gap. I have elsewhere characterized attitudes, feelings, and affects (including feelings so conspicuously associated with the TOT state) as a highly versatile device of information-holding, integration, orientation, and retrieval (Tsur, 1983a: 19–24; 1992, chapter 1). One of the crucial uses of this mechanism is its use as a word-retrieval device.

> We have access to a huge reservoir of words in our long-term memory, from which we retrieve with amazing ease and speed the words we are looking for. . . . It is the mechanism just described that underlies this high-efficiency retrieval device. This is indicated by the Tip-of-the-Tongue phenomenon. Here we can see the working of the word-retrieval device in slow motion. When we have a word at the tip of our tongue, we feel an "intensely active gap" in our consciousness, which is vague and formless but, at the same time, has a uniquely definite conscious character. Any delay between the anticipation and the picking out of words from semantic memory creates a state of unfulfilled readiness, and the inner aspect of that active schema is an affect. (ibid., 22–23; Tsur, 1992, chapter 1)

Until now, we have described the TOT phenomenon (and the mechanism from the disturbance of which it results) as a cognitive phenomenon par excellence. Since Freud's *Psychopathology of Everyday Life*, the TOT phenomenon has been widely associated with Freudian depth psychology. However, since the more recent experiments of Roger Brown and David MacNeill (Brown, 1970), we have to recognize that the TOT phenomenon per se is cognitive. We have here a typical cognitive process (the retrieval of words from semantic memory) that may be disrupted; this disruption is accompanied by a characteristic feeling (as mentioned). My claim is that the disruption can be effected in the service of poetic language or of psychopathology. One efficient way poetic language arouses feelings and affects is to keep semantic and phonological information in a diffuse state, that is, to prevent semantic and phonological elements from growing together into compact linguistic units. In poetic language the experienced feeling or effect is a significant regional quality of the expressed and suppressed semantic and phonetic information, whereas in the psychopathology of everyday life, the peculiar feeling is rather a corollary of the suppression of the forgotten word that reflects some conflict of wishes.

Freud's by now famous young man who forgot the word *aliquis* in Virgil's line "deplored the fact that the present generation of his people was being deprived of its rights, and like Dido he presaged that a new generation would take upon itself revenge against the oppressors. He therefore expressed the wish for posterity. In this moment he was interrupted by the contrary thought": "Do you really wish so much for posterity? That is not true. Just think in what predicament you would be if you should now receive information that you must expect pos-

terity from the quarter you have in mind. No, you want no posterity—
as much as you need it for your vengeance" (Freud, n.d.: 17).

The upshot of the foregoing discussion is as follows: both poetic
language and Freudian psychopathology of everyday life exploit the
smooth functioning of cognitive processes as well as their disruption,
each for its own purposes. Here I can do no better than repeat what I
have suggested elsewhere (Tsur, 1983a: 8–9). When we epitomize the
response to poetry as organized violence against cognitive processes,
we must understand, in the first place, those cognitive phenomena that
are being violated, or modified, as well as the *kinds* of violation we might
expect to encounter in relation to poetry. Second, it is not enough to
know that it is an organized violence; we must understand the principles of organization. Furthermore, there may also be organized violence against cognitive processes according to different, nonaesthetic
principles. The same cognitive processes are violated in the use of
poetic language and in the Tip-of-the-Tongue phenomenon. However,
the violence against this process is organized according to aesthetic
principles in the case of poetic language, whereas it is organized (and
highly organized at that) according to psychopathological principles in
the case of the TOT phenomenon (see Tsur, 1992, chapter 1).

Let us return to the way articulatory gestures and their perceived
effects are exploited for aesthetic purposes in poetic language, or for
psychopathological processes, or for social taboo systems in extralinguistic reality. This is an instance, as I have suggested, of organizing
cognitive processes according to aesthetic, or psychopathological, principles, or principles of social taboos. Let us focus our attention on the
gesture involved in articulating the apical /r/. I have suggested, following Fónagy's analysis (but disagreeing with him to some extent), that
it may be one of several gestures (including phallic erection and erect
menacing finger), the perceived quality of which is a mood or attitude
that contains such ingredients as self-assertion and menace. I have also
suggested that none of these gestures can be regarded as the essence to
which the other two can be reduced. We have discussed at some length
the possible ways in which this perceived quality can be exploited for
poetic purposes and organized according to aesthetic principles in an
erotic and a stormy context, and I shall not repeat it here.

Now consider the case of István, a small Hungarian boy, who was
trying to overcome his suddenly increased castration fears and to resolve the conflict by developing feminine traits; he kept the /l/ as a
substitute for /r/ up to the age of six, when he began to pronounce an

/r/ very weakly rolled (Fónagy, 1983: 99). It is quite obvious I think that István's message was "Look, I have got nothing erectile, nothing that can be castrated." This, however, does not imply that the articulatory gesture per se is somehow causally related to phallic erection that must be regarded as more basic. According to the view expounded here, it is only that István's psychopathological process (castration fear, incomplete resolution of conflict) exploited the cognitive process (the articulatory gesture and its perceived effect) for its own purposes—to bring home the message—to potential castrators. This it did by disregarding the distinction between phallic erection and an erect tongue. The psychopathology resides precisely in the fact that István did not realize the two were not the same, even though they do share certain ingredients. Furthermore, this identification was maladaptive not only from the phonetic point of view, but for the purpose of escaping castration (that anybody really wanted to castrate him). This is, then, an "organized violence against cognitive processes" organized according to psychopathological principles. The only thing it has in common with the expressive use of /r/ in poetic language is that both are organized violence against the same process of attending away from the articulatory gesture to the abstract phonetic category—but violence organized according to different principles. The two organizations overlap at the single point of the articulatory gesture and its perceived effect. Hence, it would be improper to introduce the motive of thunder storms into discussions of phallic erection, or the motive of phallic erection into descriptions of thunderstorms.

A similar story could, but will not, be told here about the exploitation of articulatory gestures and their disruption for the purposes of social behavior in "women's talk" or in "sweet talk." We have, indeed, offered above an alternative explanation for replacing the /r/ in women's talk. Likewise, in our discussion of the relation between phonological regression and aesthetic effect in chapter 2, I have pointed out that the mere phonological regression in sweet talk, for instance, or regression to nonsense talk, is of no aesthetic interest in itself. Such kinds of talk may assume aesthetic interest only when they are exploited in accordance with principles of aesthetic organization. Otherwise, they are to be regarded as mere deliberate infantilism, and of no aesthetic consequence.

All this, however, does not imply that "the violence against cognitive processes" as organized according to poetic principles and according to psychopathological principles cannot interfere with one another. Freud himself, in his *Psychopathology of Everyday Life*, provides an example, originally reported by Brill, which can be construed as an instance of such a mutual interference (n.d.: 18–20). It concerns the relation of cognitive processes and psychopathological processes; but being focused on a piece of poetry, it also provides insight into the mutual interference of psychopathological processes and poetic language. A young woman misquoted four lines from Keats's "Ode to Apollo" as

> In thy Western house of gold
> > Where thou livest in thy state,
> Bards, that once sublimely told
> > Prosaic truths that came too late.

The correct lines read as follows (the forgotten words and those replaced by others are italicized):

> In thy western *halls* of gold
> > *When* thou *sittest* in thy state,
> Bards, that *erst* sublimely told
> > *Heroic deeds, and sang of fate.* . . .

Significantly, the young woman could not recall at first on what occasion she memorized these lines. But she remembered it after Brill's suggestion: "Judging by the conversation, it would seem that this poem is intimately associated with the idea of over-estimation of personality of one in love. Have you perhaps memorized this poem when you were in such a state?" The upshot of the ensuing story is as follows:

> Everything went well for a few months, when she suddenly received word that her Apollo, for whom she had memorized these lines, had eloped with and married a very wealthy young woman. A few years later she heard that he was living in a Western city, where he was taking care of his father-in-law's interests.
>
> The misquoted lines are now quite plain. The discussion about overestimation of personality among lovers unconsciously recalled for her a disagreeable experience, when she herself overestimated the personality of the man she loved. She thought he was a god, but he turned out to be even worse than the average mortal. The episode could not come to the surface because it was determined by very disagreeable and painful thoughts, but the unconscious

variations in the poem plainly showed her present mental state. The poetic expressions were not only changed to prosaic ones, but they clearly alluded to the whole episode. (ibid., 19–20)

I submit that here, too, the unconscious processes make efficient use of some of the commonest cognitive processes (unearthed since by cognitive science). Let us consider, first, some of the more trivial replacements of the misquotation: *house* for *halls*, *livest* for *sittest*, and *once* for *erst*. How would a computer program (that cannot be credited with an unconscious mind) handle such a passage? In Roger Schank's version of artificial intelligence, it would recode it, first of all, into a representation by semantic primitives—what Schank would call an "interlingua," based on his system of "conceptual dependency" (see, for example, Schank, 1976). After this conceptual processing, the program could answer, in the question-answering mode, not only such questions as "What did bards tell about?" but also "What did ancient poets sing about?" In the translating mode, the program would not directly search for the target-language equivalent of Keats's words, but would generate *from this interlingua* a text that is roughly equivalent to the original, in French, or Spanish, or Chinese (in practice, the program—like so many intelligent readers—may have difficulties with the extraordinary complexity of the syntax, but in principle this is how it works with news items, for instance).

Now, in the paraphrasing mode, with regard to the more trivial replacements mentioned, we might expect the program to do exactly what the young woman did—substitute *house* for *halls*, *livest* for *sittest*, and *once* for *erst*. Here, too, the program would have recourse to the interlingua representation of the text and generate another English text, much in the way it generated foreign-language texts. Faced with the semantic primitives constituting highly specific words, we might expect it to pick out their more general synonyms. This is exactly how flesh-and-blood people understand texts, store them in, and retrieve them from long-term memory. We can remember only for a short time the exact words in which we received a certain piece of information. After a few seconds we recode it into a deep-structure representation, more suitable for long-term memory storage (see Tsur, 1983a: 9–12; Tsur, 1992, chapter 1). After some time, we cannot even tell in what language we received a specific piece of information. When asked, "What did the man tell you a week ago?," we usually generate, "by rule," a new text from our own interlingua representation unless we considered the message so important that we memorized it word for word. An intermediary possibility between word-for-word memorizing and the generation-by-rule of a new text from the interlingua would be to add to the interlingua-representation of words like *erst* such indices as [+ARCHAIC] or [+POETIC]. So, when generating by rule a new text from long-term memory representation, a word may be picked out that has these features, perhaps the word *erst* itself, or perhaps the phrase *of yore*.

To account for the performance of Brill's young woman, we must consider, following Liberman et al., one more issue, which I have elsewhere discussed at greater length.

> Liberman and his collaborators conceive of systems of versification as of a kind of secondary codes. "For a literate society the function of verse is primarily esthetic, but for preliterate societies, verse is a means of transmitting verbal information of cultural importance with a minimum of paraphrase. The rules of verse are, in effect, an addition to phonology which requires that recalled material not only should preserve the semantic values of the original, but should also conform to a specific, rule-determined phonetic pattern." (Tsur, 1983a: 12; see also Tsur, 1992, chapter 1; Liberman et al., 1972)

In the case of Brill's young woman, the psychopathological process consisted in interfering with this interference in recoding, partially relinquishing the restrictions on versification. In this way her cognitive functioning conformed more closely to the normal course of communication and remembering. Instead of remembering the prosodic organization as embodied in this specific piece of poetry, she encoded it as an additional rule for generating again the text from long-term memory as the rules or indices [+TROCHAIC METRE] and [+RHYME SCHEME: *gold, state, told, -ate*]. On the other hand, she systematically omitted such possible indices as [+ARCHAIC] or [+POETIC]. The upshot of my discussion is this: The mechanism responsible for the misquotation of Keats's lines has two facets, cognitive and psychopathological. The cognitive facet is the commonest possible in the normal course of communication, most typically simulated by artificial intelligence programs. Here, however, the normalization results in relaxing the versification rules that restrict the normal recoding of the surface-structure representation into deep-structure representation. What is out of the way in this example is the unconscious mind's exploitation of the normal cognitive

processes for its psychopathological purposes. The fact that "the poetic
expressions were changed to prosaic ones" becomes significant in the
unconscious attempt to express the repressed episode and, at the same
time, avoid "disagreeable and painful thoughts." There is a tendency
to use as general terms as possibly suitable when generating by rule
a surface-structure representation from a deep-structure representation. This tendency suited the purposes of the young woman's unconscious mind, interested—for its own psychopathological reasons—in
turning a poetic text into a more prosaic one.

To be sure, such kinds of substitutions may occur for stylistic reasons
too. When Keats revised his "La Belle Dame Sans Merci," he relied—
more consciously though—on the same kind of indices when changing
the first line from

O what can ail thee, Knight at arms . . .

to

Ah, what can ail thee, wretched wight . . .

We rarely encounter *wight* outside Spenser's *Faerie Queene,* and it
seems to be introduced here to increase the archaic effect of the poem;
even the substitution of *Ah* for *O* may serve to heighten poetic diction.
And we may expect to encounter the same kind of stylistic changes
in the opposite direction. All this, however, has nothing to do with
motives like those attributed to Brill's acquaintance, which should not
be dragged into the poem's context.

The misquotation of the last line (the one most telling from the
psychoanalytic point of view) cannot be accounted for in this way. Notwithstanding, it can be accounted for by assuming that the unconscious
psychopathological process, having removed the restrictions of versification on recoding, exploits an ongoing cognitive process at a different
level of information processing. To explain this we have to turn to Bartlett's discussion of schemata involved in the perception and remembering of situations.

> An individual does not normally take such a situation detail by
> detail and meticulously build up the whole. In all ordinary in-
> stances he has an overmastering tendency simply to get a general
> impression of the whole; and, on the basis of this, he constructs
> the probable detail. . . . The construction that is effected is the
> sort of construction that would justify the observer's "attitude."

(Bartlett, 1932: 206–7; see Tsur, 1983a: 21–22; see also Tsur, 1992, chapter 1)

Here the unconscious mind had its way by interfering with the cognitive process at the attitude level. By modifying the young woman's attitude toward the poem, the construction of the probable detail results in an utterly different fourth line. "Prosaic truths that came too late" expresses the young woman's attitude toward the occasion of memorizing Keats's lines; but here it also affected the attitude that served to reconstruct the lines themselves from memory. In other words, the two kinds of attitude were not kept properly separated.

Here, too, the line is constructed in accordance with the prosodic rule memorized: the fourth line deviates from the preceding lines in being iambic; it begins with a trisyllabic word and ends with the sounds -*ate*. The substitution of *where* for *when*, too, can be explained only by assuming that, once having removed the poetic restrictions on the recoding of the text, one must construct, again, the probable detail "by rule."

Psychological Explanation and Literary Study

Contrary to what may be inferred from my arguments, I am a great believer in psychoanalytic theory. However, I also believe that one must know the limitations of its application in literary theory and criticism. There seems to be good evidence that Freud himself believed so. At any rate, in the first paragraph of his "Dostoevsky and Parricide" he bluntly states: "Before the problem of the creative artist analysis must, alas, lay down its arms" (1962: 98). To be sure, we are dealing here with nothing as impenetrable as "the problem of the creative artist." But we are dealing with a domain where the application of psychological theory is seriously limited; and one must be aware of this limitation. Indeed, some of the greatest theorists seem to disapprove of it all in all. "The psychology of the reader, however interesting in itself and useful for pedagogical purposes, will always remain outside the object of literary study.... Anarchy, skepticism, a complete confusion of values is the result of every psychological theory, as it must be unrelated either to the structure or the quality of a poem" (Wellek and Warren, 1956: 135).

It should be noticed that when Wellek and Warren say "every psychological theory," it includes Fónagy's psychoanalytical approach and my own cognitive approach alike. Wellek and Warren's position was formulated in the early 1940s. I cannot dispute its justification in the light of

Reader Response Criticism that since then has developed and in recent years gathered enormous momentum. I only wish to place the issue in the double perspective of the use of critical terms and of psychological reductionism—both as handled in my earlier writings on Cognitive Poetics. In an article on critical terms and insight (Tsur, 1983c; also Tsur, 1992, chapter 21) I have argued that theoretical statements cannot be directly applied to particular poetic texts. If one wishes to apply theories to texts so as to illuminate the texts (rather than illustrate the theories), one must do so via some critical terms that have considerable *descriptive contents*. Conversely, a descriptive term can yield insight only when used in conjunction with some theoretical framework or model (sometimes only implicit in the discussion). Thus, theoretical models and frameworks (including psychological theories) serve as *commonplaces*—in the rhetorical sense of the term. "The great virtue of commonplaces is that one may appeal to them, in order to justify certain arguments on a lower level of generality. In order for the contribution of a piece of literary criticism to be informative, it must suggest some conclusion on that less general level of argument" (Tsur, 1983c: 5–6).

One crucial use of psychological theories in literary criticism is to justify the attribution of some perceived emotional quality to a poem (when Wellek and Warren speak of "the quality of a poem," they mean "character with respect to excellence" and not, as here, "perceptual quality"). A second crucial use is that psychological theories may help to generate critical terms with new descriptive contents, or further articulate the descriptive contents of old terms. At the end of this chapter I shall compare Fónagy's psychoanalytic and my own cognitive treatment of the sound patterns in a poem by Attila József. I shall argue that the psychoanalytic explanation does fulfil the first, the commonplace, function of psychological theories. In respect to descriptive contents, however, it does little more than reiterate those perceptual qualities that have been perceived and described by critics and laymen for centuries. In this respect I claim advantage for the theoretical framework propounded here: it suggests descriptive contents for critical terms by means of which one may account for intuitions concerning perceptual qualities in specific poetic texts and make meaningful distinctions between them, on the one hand, and, on the other, account for the combinational potential of sound patterns, potential that could not be described and accounted for with the help of older terms. All this does not imply, of course, that the psychoanalytical framework is unsuitable for articulating descriptive terms; it just happens that the cognitive framework has already proved its capacity in this respect. Still, cognitive theory seems somewhat preferable in this respect: perceptual processes (which are cognitive processes) most suitably account for perceptual qualities of aesthetic objects.

I have elsewhere defended Cognitive Poetics against the charge of reductionism or, in Burke's term, "essentialism" (Tsur, 1983a: 5–7; 1992, chapter 21) and shall not repeat it here. I have argued with Fodor (1979: 9–26) and Polányi (1967) that using the processes in the domains of the lower sciences one cannot predict, or explain, the nature of processes in the domains of the higher sciences (for example, explain from chemical processes the nature of physiological processes; from physiological processes the nature of psychological processes; or from psychological processes the nature of poetic processes). I adopted Polányi's conception (1967: 40) that what we have here is not a mere chain of subordinations; it is controlled by "the principle of marginal control," that is, the control that the organizational principle of a higher level exercises on the particulars forming its lower level; the successive working principles control the boundary left indeterminate on the next lower level. "Moreover, each lower level imposes restrictions on the one above it, even as the laws of nature restrict the practicability of conceivable machines; and again, we may observe that a higher operation may fail when the next lower operation escapes from its control" (ibid., 41). This is precisely where one part of my answer to Wellek and Warren resides on behalf of both Cognitive Poetics and psychoanalytic explanation. I have repeatedly characterized the response to poetry as "the organized violence against cognitive processes." Throughout chapter 1, I accounted for the perceived effects of the speech sounds that I have called "the poetic mode of speech perception" in terms of a *delay* in recoding the acoustic stream of information into the phonetic stream of information.

One basic assumption of Cognitive Poetics is that in the poetic mode some disturbance or delay occurs in the smooth functioning of some cognitive process. The same may be true, mutatis mutandis, of the disruption of some depth-psychological process. This delay or disturbance usually has a unique conscious quality that may constitute the basis of some perceived aesthetic quality. This aesthetic quality need not—moreover, cannot—be learned; one may, however, directly experience it. As for the disruption of depth-psychological processes as the source of aesthetic qualities, elsewhere I have argued, for example, that the grotesque quality results from such an interference with certain defense mechanisms. "The ridiculous," in Kenneth Burke's words, "equips us by impiety as we refuse the threat its authority" (1957: 52a), whereas the sublime, or the pitiful, or the horrible, do "allow the threat its authority." In other words, in the presence of the ridiculous the perceiver has a feeling of superiority and relative freedom, whereas in the presence of the sublime, the pitiful, and the horrible he has a feeling of smallness, helplessness, or even of being trapped. The sense of confusion and emotional disorientation associated with the grotesque results from an interference with the smooth operation of these defense mechanisms, preventing the system from settling in any one of these mutually exclusive emotional states. The grotesque occurs when poetic competence exploits the failure of these lower-level mechanisms to function properly (see Tsur, 1983c: 28–29; 1992, chapter 16). On closer inspection, then, this process turns out to be the one by way of which psychology becomes relevant to the study of literature; it imparts descriptive contents to critical terms, or it offers commonplaces for critical arguments—and all this without being vulnerable to the charge of reductionism.

So the proof of the pudding remains in the eating. In what follows, I shall consider at some length a stanza by the great Hungarian poet, Attila József, discussed by Fónagy. I shall attempt to show that psychoanalytic theory in Fónagy's discussion does properly fulfill the commonplace function of psychological theories, but its descriptive contents are less than adequately informative. I shall offer an alternative, cognitive reading, which, I claim, makes its contribution on the commonplace and the descriptive level.

A Test Case

In this section I propose to briefly compare the merits of the cognitive approach advocated here with those of the psychoanalytic approach in relation to one of Fónagy's own examples. With respect to the study of the expressiveness of sound patterns, the procedure of Cognitive Poetics can be characterized as follows. First, it begins by considering the perceived effects of sounds. Second, it attempts to account for these effects by isolating certain perceptual features of the sound stimulus or the articulatory gestures that produced them. Third, this procedure would help to determine the sound's (sometimes conflicting) combinational potential. Fourth, it would point at possible combinations of the sound with other (semantic or thematic) aspects of the poem. Fónagy's psychoanalytic explanation proceeds as follows. It also begins with the same perceived effects of sounds; then it points at some relevant articulatory gestures; then it relates the articulatory gestures with the psychoanalytic theory of the individual's psychodynamic development. Thus, for instance, the /k/ sound is hard and unpleasant because the relevant articulatory gestures are closely related to the effort required by anal excretion. For this explanation, Fónagy draws upon an unpublished paper by the Hungarian psychoanalyst István Hollós, in which a hypothesis concerning the "sado-anal investment" of the velar consonants and vowels is put forward.

> One of Hollós's main arguments is the proximity of their place of articulation to the gastric tube; another argument is the frequent occurrence of velar stops in words related in "infant language" . . . directly or indirectly to anal functions, beginning with the word *kaka*. This hypothesis is strongly corroborated by the functional correspondence of the two sphincters of the digestive tube. Thus, for instance, the glottal closure allows to exert a strong pressure on the diaphragm, and indirectly upon the intestines. . . . (1983: 90)

These are the reasons I find the cognitive approach preferable. First, intuitively, the immediately sensed perceptual qualities of the speech sounds have to do with their perceived effects (this is almost a tautology); Cognitive Poetics attempts to focus attention on these perceptual qualities, whereas psychoanalytic explanation deemphasizes them (to say the least), or even directs attention away from them one step farther. Second, cognitive poetics does not stop with explaining the perceived effects of sounds, but proceeds to determine their combinational potential. These potentials are highly versatile and offer subtle cues to account for the contribution of sound patterns to the poem's total effect, without grossly interfering with its thematic structure. The psychoanalytic explanation, at best, stops at accounting for the perceived effects of sounds, or, rather than explaining poems, it uses poems to document psychoanalytic theory. At worst, it reduces the infinite variety of poems to a small number of themes of psychoanalytic relevance; alternatively, it introduces such themes into the poem, distorting its meaning (to be sure, Fónagy represents psychoanalytic explanation at its best). In other words, in harmony with one of Ehrenzweig's (1967) central assumptions, psychoanalytic theory is better suited to deal with the contents of works of art, whereas cognitive theory is better suited to deal with artistic shape.

To substantiate some of these claims, I will closely consider one of Fónagy's examples. Fónagy remarks that "oral stops interrupt the stream of sounds into small segments, and re-establish the relationship between the stream of sounds and the anal products" (92–93). As one of his examples, he quotes lines 3–4 from the following stanza by Attila József:

> Íme, itt a költeményem.
> Ez a második sora.
> K betűkkel szól keményen,
> címe: "Költőnk és Kora."
> úgy szállong a semmi benne,
> mintha valaminek lenne
> a pora.

> (Lo, here is my poem.
> This is its second line.
> With K letters it sounds hard,
> its title is: "Our Poet and His Age."
> In it, the nothing is hovering about,
> as if it were something's
> dust.)

Fónagy also remarks in a footnote that József may have been acquainted with Hollós's work. To be sure, in a later stanza of this poem there is an explicit allusion to Freudian theory:

> Nem valóság, nem is álom,
> úgy nevezik: szublimálom
> ösztönöm.

> (Neither reality, nor dream,
> it is called: I sublimate
> my instinct.)

Notwithstanding that, there seems to be such a widespread intercultural concord concerning the relative hardness of velar stops among unsophisticated informants who may have no acquaintance with scientific theories, psychoanalytic or cognitive—one need not credit such a sensitive poet as József as being acquainted with any theory of sound symbolism. My claim is that lines 3–4 prove, or bear witness to, one thing: that József too, like almost everybody else, perceived the velar stops as relatively hard.

If we compare lines 3–4 to lines 5–7, we become aware of a pronounced contrast between the accumulation of voiceless velar stops in the former and the accumulation of nasals and liquids in the latter. I submit that this contrast can satisfactorily and fruitfully be accounted for by the hypotheses put forward in chapter 1 in terms of such oppositions as HIGHLY~LOWLY encoded, ABRUPT~CONTINUOUS, PERIODIC~APERIODIC, COMPACT~DIFFUSE. The stops are the most highly encoded speech sounds (that is, only the abstract category and little or no precategorical sensory information reaches awareness); they are abrupt; compared to voiced stops, periodicity (voice onset) begins in voiceless stops relatively late; velar stops, as opposed to dentals and labials, are compact rather than diffuse. These properties render /k/ the archetypal hard sound in that it is abrupt, that the sound energy impinging on the ear is concentrated in a relatively narrow area of the sound spectrum,[2] and that no rich precategorical sensory information reaches consciousness. By contrast, the nasals and liquids of lines 5–7 are the least encoded consonants (that is, some rich precategorical sensory information does reach consciousness); they are continuous and periodical. Thus, in the nasals and liquids of lines 5–7 a relatively large amount of diffuse and rich precategorical sensory information reaches consciousness. This is, according to the hypothesis expounded in chapter 1, the source of the perceived softness of these sounds. Further, as we have noted, there are some less clear-cut instances of sounds that are double-edged: some of their perceptual features count toward hardness and some toward softness. Thus, one may presume that in such a soft phonetic context, in the voiced labials of *benne* and *valaminek*, the diffuseness of the labial feature, the periodicity of the voiced feature, and the continuousness of the fricative feature are emphasized, the other features being deemphasized.

Before going into the contribution of this phonetic contrast to the overall effect of the stanza, I must briefly describe some of its semantic aspects. The verb *szállong* means, roughly, "hover about" and requires for a subject a noun that denotes a diffuse, shapeless entity (such as

2. "In /k, g/ spectral energy is concentrated, whereas in /t, d/, and /p, b/ is spread, with an emphasis on lower frequencies in /p, b/ and on higher frequencies in /t, d/" (Jakobson and Waugh, 1979: 103). Velar stops "display a stronger concentration of explosion" than labials and dentals (ibid., 100–101).

dust or *fog*), with an emphasis on aimlessness and on the separate movement of its particles. *Nothing* is an intellectual abstraction, denoting a
total absence of existence of any sort. The verb *szállong* turns it into
a perceptual entity, so to speak, by transferring to it the energy and
movement of *hover about*, along with such features as aimlessness and
diffuseness. The result is the perception of an intense presence detached from all the senses. The ensuing simile adds a quite complex
effect. Suppose that it said "as if it were dust"; it would have merely
reinforced this intense quality of the moving diffuse particles. But *dust*
appears here in a second perspective too: *something's dust*. *Something* is
a straightforward antonym of *nothing*. Again, suppose the simile said:
"as if it were something" (which may well be suggested by the order
of words), it would suggest a straightforward conversion of one absolute to its opposite. As the simile stands, it suggests some perceptible
dust, and some invisible *something*, whose mode or universe of existence is unknown. Thus, the fusion of the supersensuous *nothing* and
the barely perceptible *dust* is perceived as the undifferentiated, diffuse
sign of an inaccessible, unknown, "more real" reality. In other words,
we have here an immediate experiencing of "meaningfulness without
meaning." I submit, then, that we subliminally perceive some dense
texture of diffuse energy and rich precategorical sensory information
by way of perceiving the phonetic categories dominant in lines 5–7; and
that this diffuse, rich precategorical sensory information becomes part
of the overall effect of these lines, amplifying—not merely echoing—
the diffuse, dense, gestalt-free, and thing-free quality generated by the
semantic texture. This may be the reason that some native speakers of
Hungarian perceive some powerful magic in the effect of these lines.[3]

   This chapter has been devoted to methodological problems, mainly

---

3. The Hungarian Marxist ideologist Márton Horváth wrote about another poem by
Attila József ("On a Poet"): "He learnt everything that could be learnt from bourgeois
poetry. He learnt from the opposite extreme, from those who pursue artistic form for
form's sake, from Babits's group too, but in Babits's language, proving that his poem
does not voice the bad poet's envy" (Horváth, 1946: 38 [for an illuminating example, see
above, in chapter 2, Babits's "Sad Poem"]). Could this stanza, too, be a parody of the kind
of decadent poetry that uses virtuoso formal devices but *says* nothing? This may well be
true; still, two remarks seem to be pertinent here. First, what a Marxist ideologist calls
saying nothing may turn out on closer inspection to be an emotional atmosphere or the
indication of some intensive, supersensuous presence. Second, Attila József brilliantly
deploys here the formal devices in question and achieves the effect of the allegedly paro-
died poems in a way that is by no means inferior to the originals. The object of our
inquiry is how such effects are achieved.

to a consideration of the relative virtues of psychoanalytic and cognitive explanation in matters concerning the perceptual qualities and emotional symbolism of speech sounds. One relevant consideration has concerned the issue of essentializing and proportionalizing strategies. Another consideration has concerned the relationship between critical terms and theoretical models. It has been argued that critical terms receive their significance from an appropriate theoretical framework, whereas theoretical models can be applied meaningfully only via some critical terms with considerable descriptive contents. I have used the notorious alliterative patterns of a stanza by Attila József as the touchstone for the psychoanalytic and the cognitive approaches to the expressiveness of sound patterns in poetry. It has been found that both approaches offer an elaborate framework to which one may appeal to render his critical terms meaningful. However, the cognitive—but not the psychoanalytic—approach was found to offer critical terms with sufficient descriptive contents to make meaningful distinctions between, or within, poems, without introducing information relevant to the theory, but not to the poetic text.

To conclude my comparison between the two possible psychological approaches to the same sound patterns, one point remains that I have not clarified satisfactorily. I have just argued that both the cognitive and psychoanalytic approaches offer some highly elaborate theoretical framework, within which it is possible to account for the perceived hardness of voiceless velar stops. The psychoanalytic approach relies on the "proximity of their place of articulation to the gastric tube" and "the functional correspondence of the two sphincters of the digestive tube." The cognitive approach relies on the fact that in relation to the voiceless velar stops, "only the abstract category, and little or no precategorical sensory information reaches awareness." To this we might add a third, more purely phonetic explanation offered above in note 1: "In /k, g/ spectral energy is concentrated, whereas in /t, d/ and /p, b/ is spread." My position may be criticized because I have produced no criteria or arguments with reference to which of these theoretical frameworks could be preferred. One could answer to this criticism that all three accounts could be simultaneously valid on different levels of explanation. In this case, however, one should expect me to produce some kind of a "meta-explanation" as to how these three very different explanations could be valid at one and the same time, or imply one another (very much in the way I have offered a model to account for the ways in which psychopathological and aesthetic processes disrupt the cognitive processes, for different purposes). The only reasonable (in the sense of "capable of being reasoned") ground for preferring the cognitive or psychoanalytic model is, then, practical. In literary theory one should prefer theoretical models that offer critical terms that have some clearly articulated descriptive contents, with the help of which fine, meaningful distinctions can be made between, or within, poems without introducing too much external information into the text. These distinctions are also expected to determine the combinational potential of the units of poetry (in our case, the phonetic units). This does not necessarily load the dice a priori to the advantage of cognitive explanation; but it certainly presents a challenge to psychoanalytic criticism.

References

Arnheim, Rudolf. 1967. *Art and Visual Perception*. London: Faber.

Bartlett, Frederick C. 1932. *Remembering*. Cambridge: Cambridge University Press .

Bierwisch, Manfred. 1970. "Poetics and Linguistics," in Donald C. Freeman (ed.), *Linguistics and Literary Style*. New York: Holt & Rinehart.

Boon, James A. 1972. *From Symbolism to Structuralism: Lévi-Strauss in a Literary Tradition*. New York: Harper & Row.

Brady, Susan, Donald Shankweiler, and Virginia Mann. 1983. "Speech Perception and Memory Coding in Relation to Reading Ability." *Journal of Experimental Child Psychology* 35: 345–67.

Brown, Roger. 1968. *Words and Things*. New York: The Free Press.

———. 1970. "The 'Tip of the Tongue' Phenomenon," in *Psycholinguistics: Selected Papers* (274–303). New York: The Free Press.

Burke, Kenneth. 1957a. *The Philosophy of Literary Form*. New York: Vintage.

———. 1957b. "Freud—and the Analysis of Poetry," in Burke (1957a: 221–50).

———. 1957c. "On Musicality in Verse," in Burke (1957a: 296–304).

Burnshaw, Stanley. 1964. *The Poem Itself*. Harmondsworth: Pelican.

Chadwick, C. 1960. *Études sur Rimbaud*. Paris.

Chatman, Seymour, ed. 1971. *Literary Style: A Symposium*. London: Oxford University Press .

Clark, Herbert H., and Eve V. Clark. 1977. *Psychology and Language: An Introduction to Psycholinguistics*. New York: Harcourt, Brace & Jovanovich.

Cooper, William E., and John Robert Ross. 1975. "Word Order," in Robin E. Grossman, James San, and Timothy J. Vance (eds.), *Papers from the Parasession on Functionalism* (63–111). Chicago: Chicago Linguistic Society.

Crowder, Robert G. 1982a. "A Common Basis for Auditory Sensory Storage in Perception and Immediate Memory." *Perception & Psychophysics* 31: 477–83.

———. 1982b. "Disinhibition of Masking in Auditory Sensory Memory." *Memory & Cognition* 10: 424–33.

D'Andrade, Roy Godwin. 1980. "The Cultural Part of Cognition," address given to the 2nd annual Cognitive Science Conference, New Haven, Conn.

Delattre, Pierre, Alvin M. Liberman, F. S. Cooper, and L. J. Gerstman. 1952. "An Experimental Study of the Acoustic Determinants of Vowel Color." *Word* 8: 195–210.

Ehrenzweig, Anton. 1965. *The Psychoanalysis of Artistic Vision and Hearing*. New York: Braziller.

Étiemble, René. 1968. *Le Sonnet des Voyelles*. Paris: Gallimard.

Fodor, Jerry A. 1979. *The Language of Thought*. Cambridge: Harvard University Press.

Fónagy, Iván. 1961. "Communication in Poetry." *Word* 17: 194–218.

――――. 1971. "The Functions of Vocal Style," in Chatman (1971: 159–76).

――――. 1983. *La Vive Voix: Essais de Psycho-phonétique*. Paris: Payot.

Freud, Sigmund. N.d. *Psychopathology of Everyday Life*. New York: Mentor.

――――. 1962. "Dostoevsky and Parricide," in René Wellek (ed.), *Dostoevsky*. Englewood Cliffs, N.J.: Prentice-Hall.

Fromkin, Victoria A. 1973. "Slips of the Tongue." *Scientific American* 229, no 6: 110–17.

Fry, D. B. "Speech Reception and Perception," in John Lyons (ed.), *New Horizons in Linguistics* (29–52). Harmondsworth: Pelican.

Genette, Gérard. 1966. *Figures*. Paris: Du Seuil ("Tel Quel").

Glucksberg, Sam, and Joseph H. Danks. 1975. *Experimental Psycholinguistics*. Hillsdale, N.J.: Erlbaum.

Gombrich, E. H. 1984. *The Sense of Order: A Study in the Psychology of Decorative Art*. Oxford: Phaidon.

Halle, Morris. 1978. "Knowledge Unlearned and Untaught: What Speakers Know About the Sounds of Their Language," in Morris Halle, Joan Bresnan, and George A. Miller (eds.), *Linguistic Theory and Psychological Reality* (294–303). Cambridge: MIT Press.

Horváth, Márton. 1946. "József Attila Költészete," in György Lukács and Márton Horváth, *József Attila* (33–67). Budapest: Szikra.

Houston, J. P. 1963. *The Design of Rimbaud's Poetry*. New Haven, Conn.: Yale University Press .

Hrushovski, Benjamin. 1968. "Do Sounds Have Meaning? The Problem of Expressiveness of Sound-Patterns in Poetry." *Hasifrut* 1: 410–20 (in Hebrew); English summary: 444.

――――. 1980. "The Meaning of Sound Patterns in Poetry: An Interaction View." *Poetics Today* 2: 39–56.

Jakobson, Roman. 1968. *Child Language, Aphasia, and Phonological Universals*. The Hague: Mouton.

――――. 1980. *Brain and Language*. Columbus, Ohio: Slavica.

Jakobson, Roman, and Linda R. Waugh. 1979. *The Sound Shape of Language*. Bloomington: Indiana University Press .

Kawasaki, Haruko. 1986. "Phonetic Explanation for Phonological Universals: The Case of Distinctive Vowel Nasalization," in Ohala and Jaeger (1986: 81–103).

Knight, Wilson G. 1965. *The Imperial Theme*. London: Methuen.

Kris, Ernst, and E. H. Gombrich. 1965. "The Principles of Caricature," in Ernst Kris, *Psychoanalytic Explorations in Art*. New York: Schocken.

Kubovy, Michael. N.d. "Two Hypotheses Concerning the Interrelation of Perceptual Spaces."

————. 1981. "Concurrent Pitch-Segregation and the Theory of Indispensable Attributes," in M. Kubovy and J. Pomerantz (eds.), *Perceptual Organization*. Hillsdale, N.J.: Erlbaum.

Langacker, Ronald W. 1987. *Foundations of Cognitive Grammar*. Stanford, Calif.: Stanford University Press.

Lever, J. 1966. *The Elizabethan Love Sonnet*. London: Methuen.

Liberman, A. M. 1970. "The Grammars of Speech and Language." *Cognitive Psychology* 1: 301–23.

Liberman, A. M., F. S. Cooper, D. P. Shankweiler, and M. Studdert-Kennedy. 1967. "Perception of the Speech Code," *Psychological Review* 74: 431–61.

Liberman, A. M., and David S. Isenberg. 1980. "Duplex Perception of Acoustic Patterns as Speech and Nonspeech." *Status Report on Speech Research* SR-62: 47–57. Haskins Laboratories.

Liberman, A. M., I. M. Mattingly, and M. T. Turvey. 1972. "Language Codes and Memory Codes," in A. W. Melton and E. Martin (eds.), *Coding Processes in Human Memory*. New York: Winston.

Liberman, Isabelle Y., and Virginia A. Mann. 1981. "Should Reading Instruction and Remediation Vary with the Sex of the Child?" *Status Report on Speech Research* SR-65: 125–43. Haskins Laboratories.

Liberman, Mark. 1979. *The Intonational System of English*. New York: Garland.

Lyons, John. 1977. *Semantics*. Cambridge: Cambridge University Press .

Mann, Virginia A. 1982. "Reading Skill and Language Skill." *Developmental Review* 4: 1–15.

Mattingly, I. G., A. M. Liberman, A. K. Syrdal, and T. Halwes. 1971. "Discrimination in Speech and Nonspeech Mode." *Cognitive Psychology* 2: 131–57.

May, Janet, and Bruno H. Repp. 1982. "Periodicity and Auditory Memory." *Status Report on Speech Research* SR-69: 145–49. Haskins Laboratories.

Meyer, Leonard B. 1956. *Emotion and Meaning in Music*. Chicago: University of Chicago Press .

Miles, Josephine. 1965. *Pathetic Fallacy in the 19th Century*. New York: Hippocrene Books.

Miller, George A., and Philip N. Johnson-Laird. 1976. *Language and Perception*. Cambridge: Harvard University Press .

Neisser, Ulric. 1976. *Cognition and Reality*. San Francisco: Freeman.

Ohala, J. John, and Jeri J. Jaeger, eds. 1986. *Experimental Phonology*. Orlando, Fla.: Academic Press.

Plessen, Jacques. 1967. *Promenade et Poésie*. Le Haye: Mouton.

Polányi, Michael. 1967. *The Tacit Dimension*. Garden City, N.Y.: Anchor Books.

Rakerd, Brad. 1984. "Vowels in Consonantal Context Are More Linguistically Perceived than Isolated Vowels: Evidence from an Individual Differences Scaling Study." *Perception & Psychophysics* 35: 123–36.

Rakerd, Brad, Alvin M. Liberman, and David Isenberg. 1981. "More on Duplex Perception of Cues for Stop Consonants." *Status Report on Speech Research* SR-65: 233–44. Haskins Laboratories.

Ratsahbi, Yehuda. 1969–70. "Love in Rabbi Shəmuel Hannagid's Poetry." *Tarbiṣ* 39: 137–69 (in Hebrew).

Reichard, G. A., R. Jakobson, and E. Werth. 1949. "Language and Synaesthesia," *Word* 5: 224–34.

Repp, Bruno H. 1983. "Against a Role of 'Chirp' Identification in Duplex Perception." *Perception & Psychophysics* 35: 89–93.

———. 1984. "Categorical Perception: Issues, Methods, Findings," in N. J. Lass (ed.), *Speech and Language: Advances in Basic Research and Practice*, 10:243–335. New York: Academic Press.

Repp, Bruno H., Christina Milburn, and John Ashkenas. 1982. "Duplex Perception: Confirmation or Fusion." *Perception & Psychophysics* 33: 333–37.

Richards, I. A. 1929. *Practical Criticism*. New York: Harvest Books.

Richer, Jean. 1972. *L'Alchimie du Verbe de Rimbaud*. Paris: Didier.

Rohrer, C. 1973. "The Treatment of the French Nasal Vowels in Generative Phonology," in Erik C. Fudge (ed.), *Phonology* (232–41). Harmondsworth: Penguin.

Rumelhart, David E. 1979. "Some Problems with the Notions of Literal Meaning," in Andrew Ortony (ed.), *Metaphor and Thought* (78–90). Cambridge: Cambridge University Press.

Schank, Roger C. 1976. "The Role of Memory in Language Processing," in Charles N. Cofer (ed.), *The Structure of Human Memory* (162–89). San Francisco: Freeman.

Shepard, Roger N. 1981. "Psychophysical Complementarity," in M. Kubovy and J. Pomerantz (eds.), *Perceptual Organization*. Hillsdale, N.J.: Erlbaum.

Spitzer, Leo. 1969. "The Muting Effect of Classical Style in Racine," in R. C. Knight (ed.), *Racine*, 117–31. London: Macmillan.

Starkie, Enid. 1961. *Arthur Rimbaud* (3rd ed.). London: Faber and Faber.

Studdert-Kennedy, Michael. 1982. "Discovering the Sound Pattern of a Language." *Contemporary Psychology* 27: 510–12.

Szerb, Antal. 1943. *A Világirodalom Története*. Budapest: Révai.

Tsur, Reuven. 1971. "A Rhetoric of Poetic Qualities." Unpublished dissertation, Sussex University.

———. 1975. "Two Critical Attitudes: Quest for Certitude and Negative Capability." *College English* 36: 776–88.

———. 1977. *A Perception-Oriented Theory of Metre*. Tel Aviv: Porter Institute for Poetics and Semiotics.

———. 1978. "Emotion and Emotional Qualities in Poetry." *Psychocultural Review*: 165–80.

———. 1983a. *What Is Cognitive Poetics?* Tel Aviv: Katz Research Institute for Hebrew Literature.

———. 1983b. *Poetic Structure, Information-Processing and Perceived Effects: Rhyme and Poetic Competence*. Tel Aviv: Katz Research Institute for Hebrew Literature.

———. 1983c. *Critical Terms and Insight: The Mental Dictionary of "Critical Competence."* Tel Aviv: Katz Research Institute for Hebrew Literature.

———. 1987. *On Metaphoring*. Jerusalem: Israel Science Publishers.

———. 1992. *Toward a Theory of Cognitive Poetics*. Amsterdam: Elsevier Publishers.

Ullmann, Stephen. 1957. *The Principles of Semantics*. Oxford: Blackwell.

———. 1966. *Language and Style*. Oxford: Blackwell.

Ultan, Russell. 1978. "Size-Sound Symbolism," in Joseph H. Greenberg (ed.), *Universals of Human Language*, vol. 2: *Phonology*. Stanford, Calif.: Stanford University Press .

Wellek, René, and Austin Warren. 1956. *Theory of Literature*. New York: Harcourt, Brace & Co.

Wittgenstein, Ludwig. 1976. *Philosopical Investigations*. Oxford: Blackwell.
Wright, James T. 1986. "The Behavior of Nasalized Vowels in the Perceptual Space," in
    Ohala and Jaeger (1986: 45–67).

Index

Reuven Tsur is Professor in the Department of
Hebrew literature at Tel Aviv University. He is also
Director of the Katz Research Institute for
Hebrew Literature, Tel Aviv University, where he
heads The Cognitive Poetics Project.

Library of Congress
Cataloging-in-Publication Data
Tsur, Reuven.
What makes sound patterns expressive?: the
poetic mode of speech perception / Reuven Tsur.
p. cm. — (Sound and meaning)
Rev. ed. of: How do the sound patterns know they
are expressive?
Includes bibliographical references and index.
ISBN0-8223-1164-x (alk. paper)
ISBN 0-8223-1170-4 (pbk. : alk paper)
1. Sound symbolism. 2. Speech perception. 3.
Versification.
I. Tsur, Reuven. How do the sound patterns know
they are expressive? II. Title. III. Series.
P119.T78 1992
414'.6—dc20   91–585 CIP